The Power *of* Talking Out Loud *to* Yourself

Break Through to Exciting New Levels of Success at Work and in Life

BILL WAYNE

A Possibility Press Book

The

Power

of

Talking
Out Loud

to

Yourself

BILL WAYNE

Published by
Possibility Press
possibilitypress@aol.com

Manufactured in the United States of America

Dedication

This is for you, for recognizing that your future is solely your responsibility and that you can make it great, fulfilling, and successful. Congratulations for having the courage to take the actions necessary to become the best you can be. Now go out and make the world a better place in which to live.

This book is especially dedicated to my wise and devoted wife, Dee, without whom Chapter 4 could not have been written. We have been married nearly 50 years and yet, every day, she still amazes me.

"When you talk out loud to yourself, you cause yourself to focus intently on the challenge, situation, or circumstance. This activity increases the likelihood of obtaining a desirable solution more quickly. It is easy to daydream nonproductively for an hour or two, but it only wastes time and doesn't give you the results you'd like to have. It is incredibly powerful hearing your own voice emotionally proclaiming what you intend and expect to accomplish. Talking out loud to yourself can go a long way in helping you move on."

—Bill Wayne

Contents

Shaking Hands With Your Future

"If you have built castles in the air, your
work need not be lost; that is where they should be.
Now put foundations under them."
—Henry David Thoreau—

How do you get to where you want to go? Everyone wants to live a better, happier, more enriched life, but why do so few ever realize it?

Everyone wants to do a better job of overcoming obstacles and achieving goals. After all, life is a continuous process of making choices and dealing with challenges.

We all make mistakes from time to time. The best we can do then is to learn from them and go on to a new level of living—letting go of the burden of old patterns that simply don't work for us anymore.

We would all like to smooth out the bumps on the road of life so we can move along more easily to accomplish our goals, and make our dreams come true sooner rather than later. However, some people are so overwhelmed by the bumps, ruts, and chuckholes that mistakes, challenges, and decisions bring them to a halt, leaving them in a mire of unhappiness and frustration. Their friends and family are often in similar situations and, therefore, unable to assist them.

Other people seem to travel along in life haphazardly, barely managing to arrive at a destination that is only somewhat acceptable. It's quite a bit short of their real dreams of success and happiness. Still others learn to dream and set goals, and overcome obstacles as they doggedly persist. They successfully get out from under circumstances others don't and live the lives they envision.

Well folks, everyone *can* be more successful, and this book could be an excellent tool to help you accelerate the process. The methods in this book work. I've used them for years, and continue doing so. These simple, basic procedures remain a daily part of my "tool box" as I journey toward ever greater levels of success, happiness, and fulfillment. And I can honestly say that I reach new levels of living all the time, and so can you.

This book can help you jumpstart the rest of your life's quest, no matter where you are now. Whether you are 19 or 99, if you want to become the best you can be and achieve the most you can during the rest of your life, this book can help you begin or continue on with that journey.

No doubt, you have heard the adage that *today is the first day of the rest of your life.* Every day we are all beginners for what lies ahead. Every day gives us a fresh, new opportunity to launch ourselves into new achievement and success, regardless of what our yesterdays produced or didn't. Yesterday is history and it can't be changed. Tomorrow isn't here yet, and it's promised to no one. There is only *today,* and it's ours to mold so our tomorrows can be what we'd like them to be.

But wonderful tomorrows don't come by sitting on our hands and wishing. We need to take decisive action today and all of our future todays. Every day we need to break through the obstacles that seemingly block our journey toward living the life we want.

This book is designed to help you make *breakthroughs—sudden successes that overcome obstacles to progress.* We can help ourselves do this more effectively by engaging in an innovative twist to positive self-talk—*Self-Communication Of Realistic Expectations.* I call it *SCOREing,* which is done out loud to yourself.

Now it's important to understand, right at the outset, that a realistic expectation is based on whatever you believe. If there's an old habit you'd like to stop or a new one you'd like to adopt, or something you'd like to accomplish that you don't think is "realistic," you can start by changing your belief. To begin heading toward accomplishing something you haven't done before, start believing it and you'll begin seeing it!

For example, when President Kennedy set the goal of putting a man on the moon, it was "unrealistic." In a Special Message to Congress, given on May 25, 1961, Kennedy said, "We go into space because whatever mankind must undertake, free men must fully share.... I believe that this nation should commit itself to achieving the goal, before this decade is out, of landing a man on the moon and returning him safely to the earth."

At the time Kennedy made that startling announcement, no rocket or space capsule existed that could make a lunar landing a reality. But his leadership in making that statement helped people raise their belief to where putting a man on the moon was accepted as realistic. This shift in belief can work for you too. Simply start believing that whatever you'd like to accomplish, even if at first it appears to be unrealistic, actually *is* realistic! So how can that be done?

The Power of Talking Out Loud to Yourself shows you how to take actions to help you change your thinking about something from unrealistic to realistic. This will enable you to improve your life while advancing in whatever direction you may choose. You'll learn that it's fun and easy to *SCORE*. It can be done by anyone, and a degree in rocket science is not required. All you need is faith in yourself, perseverance, and the self-discipline to perform some simple *SCOREing* approaches. And if self-discipline is a challenge, there's even a *SCOREing* approach to help you develop that as well!

Chapter 1, Part A includes more details about some powerful *SCOREing* approaches and how to implement them. Parts B and C go into greater detail about how and why you can accomplish whatever you program your mind to do—by breaking through to success by *SCOREing*. The remaining chapters contain a variety of specific *SCOREing* approach scenarios and dialogues that can be adapted to virtually any life circumstance you're likely to encounter.

To augment your *SCOREing*, you also could create an audio recording of what you say out loud to yourself, perhaps with some inspiring music in the background. You could then press "play" anytime you want to hear yourself declare what you want to change or create. Use a portable audio player with an earphone, and you won't disturb anyone. And, of course, you could also play it back in the car to and from work, when you're in the bathroom getting ready for work or bed, or other private places.

At times the book is humorous, while at others it is serious, and probably unlike any other you've ever read. So maintain a sense of humor, keep an open mind, and stay with me. These are methods you can start using today. They are doable within the framework of your current lifestyle, regardless of what that may be. You may or may not need to use everything suggested, depending on your situation. Even if a particular approach isn't useful to you, perhaps you know others who could benefit from it.

This book is about using the spoken word as a powerful tool for achieving what you deeply desire. *SCOREing* can help you enhance every area of your life, perhaps beyond your wildest dreams. In later chapters you will learn how to successfully *SCORE* in a variety of specific daily situations—from making peace after an argument, to getting a good deal when purchasing a car, and even starting and running your own business.

We all have our own ideas of fulfillment and happiness and the right to achieve our heart's desires, as long as we are willing to pursue them by helping rather than harming others. And while no one's dream is more or less important than anyone else's, the world will step aside and let anyone pass who knows where he or she is going.

This book gives you an innovative approach to positive self-talk that will help you make changes in your life—*so you can move on.* Add intention, expectation, determination, and persistence and you, too, can put a solid foundation under your dreams—by using *the power of talking out loud to yourself.*

SCORE your way to success,

Bill Wayne

"*Those who pursue their dreams are often thought of as being crazy—generally by those who aren't moving on. But don't concern yourself with that. It's their problem, not yours. This is your life, and you have the right to go after your dreams with all your might. Now let's get on with it.*"

—Bill Wayne

-1-

Talk Out Loud to Yourself and *SCORE*

"I have no yesterdays, time took them away;
Tomorrow may not be—but I have Today."
—Pearl Yeadon McGinnis—

—*Part A*—
Chewing the Rag
Talking It Over With Yourself

"Chewing the rag" is a colloquialism that means having a conversation or dialogue with someone. In other words, chit-chat.

We are going to put a little different spin on chewing the rag, to make you aware of an extraordinarily powerful skill you can use to achieve your goals. The great news is you already possess this skill. You just may not realize it and, probably, have not yet learned how to use it.

You are going to learn to say certain words out loud to yourself. That's right—you will talk out loud (chew the rag) *to yourself*—while you are alone, of course! If you are unable to speak due to a physical

11

disability but you can sign, talk to yourself in sign language. If you are unable to speak or sign, talk to yourself by writing. If you are unable to speak, sign, or write, speak to yourself in your mind, using the same words as though you were talking out loud to yourself. Where there's a will there's a way. Anyone can use this book. No excuse! You can help yourself if you really want to. The *SCOREing* Approach dialogues are written as though someone is speaking to him or herself out loud, which is the way I do it and teach it. Why? The spoken word is an incredibly powerful tool for influencing the mind, the actions you take, and the results you get. Just think back to your schooldays when you had to learn a poem or a passage from Shakespeare so you could recite it in front of the class. Didn't you learn it by practicing it out loud to yourself?

Some of my favorite places to chew the rag with myself are in the bathroom, alone in the car, or any other place where I'm alone. If I have the need to chew the rag while others are around, I either whisper discretely to myself or do it mentally. Otherwise, some people may think I am a little "off center," and I certainly don't want to do anything that would confirm their suspicions!

Those who pursue their dreams are often thought of as being crazy—generally by those who *aren't* moving on. But don't concern yourself with that. It's *their* problem, not yours. This is *your* life, and you have the right to go after your dreams with all your might. So, let's get on with it.

You'll learn to chew the rag, with yourself—to blast through obstacles, achieve goals, improve your life, and gain more happiness and success. You can even chew the rag to help make your dreams come true. Now, since chewing the rag would be a rather cumbersome phrase to use over and over again, I will use the acronym *SCORE*, as defined earlier, to convey the meaning and make it easier for you.

Let's say you have an expectation or goal. For example: You want to have a better relationship with your spouse or boss; or perhaps you want to overcome a fear or negative habit. Use **S***elf-***C***ommunication* **O***f* **R***ealistic Expectations* to help yourself succeed. Accelerate your success by *SCOREing,* and unleash the awesome power you have to talk yourself into, or out of, virtually anything.

Now let's let the fun begin. And folks, it really *is* fun. In fact, it's a hoot!

—*Part B*—
The Mouth That Roared
What SCOREING Is All About

At some time or other we have all heard or used the term "psyched up." We might have said something like…

"I psyched myself up for the job interview."
"I knew it would be a difficult task, so I psyched myself up for it."
"I'm all psyched up for the presentation."
"I'm all psyched up about my dream!"

So what does "psyched up" mean in this context? It usually means we've had a little mental pep talk with ourselves about some situation of interest or concern, and we're excited about it.

You may be apprehensive about some event, situation, or challenge so you tell yourself you will be confident, unafraid, strong, well prepared, in control, mentally alert, and so forth. You are the coach preparing your team for the big game but, in this case, you are both the coach *and* the team. You're holding a pep rally with yourself to help yourself get moving.

The amazing thing is that this *really* works—but only *when you use it!* Why? What is really happening here? Is it magic? Is it self-delusion? Is it coincidence? No, it is none of these things. It is something else entirely. It is something so simple, so natural that we don't give it a second thought.

If we did give it any thought, we'd say, "Wow! I have a great power inside me. I want to learn how to use it effectively so my life will be better. I want to be a winner all the time!"

You may be in business and want to improve your skills so you can be more successful. You may have a desire to be more effective in interacting with others and build better relationships. You may also want to improve your own behavior in various ways, become more self-confident, change your attitude, improve your memory, or something else.

You may need to purchase a new vehicle and want to get a great deal. You may be a supervisor, manager, or leader who'd like to be more effective. Perhaps you are an employee who wants to have a better relationship with your boss. Maybe you're a parent desiring to interact better with your spouse and children—or to have them better interact with you. We all would like to always be "at the right place at the right time." And who wouldn't like to be a bit more well-off financially?

Your mouth is a tremendous tool, and you can use it in an unusual and powerful way to bring about astounding changes in your life. You can become "the mouth that roared" using the *SCOREing* approach in a special way so you can program your mind for success. The spoken word can be exceptionally effective in programming the subconscious mind as shown by the following illustration:

After I finished basic training in the U.S. Air Force many years ago, I attended radar school. It was eight hours a day, five days a week, for 40 weeks—200 days total. Every day the instructor took roll call twice—before class started and after lunch. Usually there was a different instructor every week. On the first day, the instructor started the roll call. As he bellowed out each last name in alphabetical order, the student would respond with, "Present!"

"Alberts!"

"Present!"

"Bostick!"

"Present!"

The instructor proceeded with the roll call. I knew my last name, Wayne, would be the last one called after Volker.

"Gager!"

"Present!"

"Hayne!"

No answer.

"Hayne!" the instructor called out again.

Still no answer.

I looked around the room wondering who in the world Hayne was.

"Hayne is absent," the sergeant muttered and he proceeded with the roll call, finishing with Volker, not calling my name.

I raised my hand and said, "Sergeant you didn't call my name, Wayne."

The sergeant quickly figured out that I was the "Hayne" on the roster who didn't answer.

"Typographical error," the sergeant replied. "I'll get it fixed."

The next day was the exact same scenario. I was still Hayne on the roster, and the instructor again vowed to get it fixed.

Every day, without exception, I was Hayne and I always responded mechanically, "Present! The name is Wayne, not Hayne."

It became a standing joke, and my buddies all started calling me Hayne.

On day 196 we got a brand new instructor, fresh out of instructor's training. Again the roster was still incorrect and we went through the usual "Not Hayne, it's Wayne" scenario with the instructor vowing to get the roster corrected. On the next day, unbeknownst to me, he finally got it right.

On day 197, the roll call went like this:

"Volker!"

"Present!"

"Wayne!"

"Not Wayne, it's Hayne!" I responded automatically without thinking.

The class roared with laughter. I had taken on the identity of "Hayne" at the subconscious level and responded accordingly. My intention wasn't to be funny. It was just a conditioned response.

The most powerful and personal identity an individual has is his or her name. Yet through the spoken word repeated hundreds of times, I had automatically been conditioned to assume another name—Hayne—when I was in the classroom environment. As crazy as it may seem, I actually thought of myself as being Hayne!

Now that can be both scary and awesome. It could be scary because you have no doubt realized that a lot of damage can be done with the spoken word. But on the flip side, it's awesome because you also understand how much good can be done with the spoken word.

When you start talking to yourself in the ways suggested in this book, your life can grow richer in every area.

—*Part C*—
Want an Intelligent Conversation?
SCORE Your Subconscious Mind

It used to be that anyone who talked out loud to him or herself was considered "not quite right in the head." As you may have witnessed, someone might make a gesture, like pointing a finger to his or her temple while making a circular motion with it, indicating that the person talking to him or herself was mixed up in the head. He or she might make a snide remark such as: "He is fifty cents short of having a dollar," "She doesn't have both oars in the water," "His pilot light blew out," "His elevator doesn't go all the way to the top," or some other similar unkind remark. (I don't recommend doing this, by the way!)

Today, things are different. It's now regarded as intelligent—by those who understand personal development and success—to purposefully talk out loud to ourselves. Until now, people have practiced positive self-talk silently in their heads, but it's not nearly as effective as talking out loud to ourselves!

It's simple. When you sincerely want to make a constructive change in your life, talk out loud to yourself in a positive way and take appropriate action. As you do, you'll find achievement at your door, pounding to get in.

We all talk to ourselves anyway, silently and perhaps out loud. So why not tell ourselves something to help us win more often in life? You'll find *SCOREing* to be a powerful mechanism to support the achievement of whatever it is you truly want. And as you are about to learn, there is good reason for this.

All of us have various wants and needs, which change as we age and grow. But some people, the more successful among us, have better defined them in terms of dreams, goals, and objectives. There are lofty goals, such as becoming wealthy. Then there are more ordinary ones, such as finding stable employment. Of course, a nearly infinite number of goals, dreams, and needs lie in between those two.

We all have within us everything we need to achieve whatever it is we want in life! We may simply need to learn how to better use these resources and the power we already possess. Successful people know how to activate and use it, either consciously or subconsciously. That is one reason why they are successful. You, too, can consciously activate your subconscious power in concert with the rest of your innate power to become a dynamo of self-motivated achievement.

Why Does *SCOREing* Work?

To answer this, let's briefly discuss mentally talking to yourself and how your subconscious mind works. Observe your thoughts and it'll be evident that you are always talking to yourself mentally about one thing or another. This mental self-talk most often concerns resolving some minor daily challenge such as balancing the budget (which may not be so minor for some!), choosing how to discuss some sensitive subject with another person, or deciding on the best approach to handle a job or business-related situation.

Occasionally, we give ourselves mental pep talks when preparing for a job interview, presentation, or similar situation. Less frequently, but more importantly, we have some major hurdle to overcome and have a silent debate about what to do. It could be something like saving your marriage, overcoming a health challenge, or dealing with a child's drug or alcohol addiction.

If you have extraordinary powers of concentration, and your mind is exceptionally well-disciplined, you can achieve good results through mental self-talk. And it works quite well when you combine it with visualizing the results you would like to have. The common challenge with mental self-talk, though, is that most people don't know how to really concentrate, lack self-discipline, or don't have a dream to focus on. Lacking any one of these may cause your results to be less than you would like. Lacking all three definitely prevents positive results from happening.

So why does mental self-talk work at all? Each of us was created with a subconscious mind—our obedient internal servant that accepts whatever it is told—no more, no less. It doesn't think or reason—it just drives us according to how we program it.

If you allow it, other people can also program your subconscious. If someone says, "You're stupid," and you choose to believe they are right, your subconscious mind accepts it as fact. Your subconscious then proceeds to alter your behavior so you do, indeed, behave stupidly. If, however, your attitude is "That may be your opinion, but I know I'm not stupid," then your subconscious will not allow you to behave stupidly.

Imagine how much harm is being done to children when parents or others constantly say negative things to them like: "You are so stupid;" "You never do anything right;" "Don't expect boys to look at you; You're so homely."

You have the power to direct your subconscious mind by using your natural thought processes. You can achieve whatever you wish by repeatedly programming your subconscious with clear, realistic, messages, by *SCOREing* on your subconscious!

Why Would Your Subconscious Take You Seriously?

Your subconscious is rarely impressed by one or two passing thoughts. Having the fleeting thought, "I want to be a millionaire," is highly unlikely to result in any changes in your income. Your subconscious mind needs to be *impressed*. It needs to be taught. You need to *effectively* let it know *exactly* what you want. And this can be done only by repetition, consistency, emotion, and clear, super-focused concentration.

Repetition is pretty much self-explanatory. You need to repeatedly express your desires to your subconscious through your self-talk, until you achieve what you want.

Consistency is a key factor which most people ignore. For example, you say you want to improve your lifestyle by building your career or business, and you self-talk that diligently for several weeks. Unfortunately, however, you allow someone to stomp on your dream, and you end up settling for a modestly paying job for the rest of your life—even though you may hate it. A week later, bored with your job, you decide what you really want to do is to sell life insurance. Then, a few weeks after that, you change your mind again—and so on and so on.

All of this indecisiveness causes your subconscious mind to become confused. You keep giving it different instructions. You have not been clear and consistent with it. So it does the only thing it can—*nothing*. If you consistently engage in this kind of changeable self-talk, your subconscious cannot possibly know what you really want. You're not getting through to it. The net effect is that your subconscious won't take you seriously. And if you ever do decide on what you really want, your subconscious mind will most likely ignore you. This is known as the infamous "crying wolf" syndrome.

So how can you more effectively perform self-communication? This is where *SCOREing* comes into play. But before you start talking out loud to yourself, you first need to think, i.e., engage in *mental* self-talk! This, quite frequently, invokes a mental picture of your desire. But then, thanks to *SCOREing*, you can go one step further. You speak the words you are thinking, they enter your mind through your ears, and your thoughts become reinforced. This is nothing less than a double whammy—two for the price of one.

Clear, super-focused concentration is vital to programming your subconscious, and talking out loud to yourself helps you create it. You know all too well how easy it is for your mind to stray from thought to thought, as it wanders aimlessly while you are thinking. That's just what our minds tend to do when we're not focusing on anything in particular. However, it is very difficult for your mind to wander when you concentrate *and* talk out loud to yourself about something specific. In order for you to speak in a targeted way, your mind can't help but stay focused—and *SCOREing* helps you do so. *Talking out loud to yourself enables you to more effectively reach your subconscious as compared to just mentally talking to yourself.*

One day, about 25 years ago, when my youngest daughter was in high school, I noticed her sitting in our living room. She was reading a book, but every few minutes she would glance up and stare into space. After about 15 minutes of this routine, my curiosity got the best of me and I asked her what she was doing.

"I am *trying* to memorize this stupid poem that I have to recite in front of the class tomorrow," she replied, sounding a little exasperated.

"Are you going to give it silently in front of the class?" I asked.

"Of course not."

"Then if you have to speak it out loud, why not memorize it out loud?" I suggested. "Doesn't that make sense?"

She countered that people would think she was loony if she talked out loud to herself. When I pointed out that only her mother and I were present, she compromised by going into another room and shutting the door. I could hear her in there reading the poem out loud to herself. Within a few minutes she came out and victoriously announced, "I've got it!"

Some of the seeds for this book were planted in my mind because of that event. During the intervening years, I have been *SCOREing* daily with great success.

Emotion is one other factor that greatly increases the effectiveness of SCOREing. The more emotion you put into your words, the more effectively you can reach and teach your subconscious. So do some playacting. Get emotional. Shout. Plead. Show anger. Show joy. Show heartfelt sincerity. Run the full gamut of emotions that would be appropriate for the particular situation in which you are *SCOREing*.

The subconscious *really* listens to emotion. With enough emotion, just one *SCOREing* session could be enough to make your subconscious take you seriously and enable you to alter your behavior immediately for results. For example, the athlete who is intensely focused and fervently charged with emotion is more likely to win a contest against all odds. Or someone frail or elderly becomes so emotionally worked up that he or she runs into a burning building and saves lives. Yes, there's tremendous power in profound emotion, especially when you utilize the power of talking out loud to yourself.

"It used to be that any-one who talked out loud to him or herself was considered 'not quite right in the head.' Today things are different. It is now regarded as intelligent—by those who understand personal development and success—to purposely talk out loud to ourselves."

—Bill Wayne

"Encourage yourself by focusing on your behavior—how you acted—instead of calling yourself names, labeling yourself, and hurting your self-esteem. When you give yourself instructions for how you want to behave in the future, do so in positive terms. If you tell yourself not to do something, your subconscious doesn't hear the not—it only hears the something! Your mind cannot focus on the opposite of an idea."

—Bill Wayne

-2-

Straighten Yourself Out and Get With the Program!

SCOREing Against Undesirable Behaviors

"It is not what he has, nor even what he does, which directly expresses the worth of a man, but what he is."
—Henri Frederic Amiel—

We all make mistakes now and then. We do or say something inappropriate, or we neglect to do or say something that *is* appropriate. Most often these mistakes are minor, but occasionally they are major.

Whether mistakes are major or minor mistakes, however, you need to deal with them effectively when they occur, or as soon afterward as possible—*and then dismiss them from your mind.* Otherwise they'll just clutter it up. There is absolutely no constructive value in dwelling on a mistake you've made. All it does is bring you down mentally. As you'll soon learn, *SCOREing* Approaches #1 and #2 can be used to empower you to handle all aspects of any mistakes you make.

It's okay, even advisable, to occasionally recall inappropriate actions and the lessons you've learned from them. It helps keep you honest, so to speak, and better able to avoid repeating the same behavioral mistakes over and over again. But this is different than dwelling on mistakes, which is counterproductive to success.

You need to deal with those things you said or did that didn't work—so you can straighten out your thinking. We all make mistakes for a variety of reasons: lack of concentration, being tired, acting too hastily, doing something without first thinking it through, exercising faulty judgment, practicing a negative habit pattern, making an excuse, or something else.

We need to give a loud, strong message to our subconscious that this is *not* the way we want to be. We want to eliminate undesirable behaviors. This process is called "straightening yourself out." The most effective way to do so is to *SCORE* by using strong, powerful words—putting as much emotion into them as you can muster.

Here are the three elements you can use to help straighten yourself out:

1. Review the mistake in detail—*out loud.*
2. Correct your behavior appropriately—*out loud.*
3. Tell yourself what remedial action you will take—*out loud.*

With regard to item 2, correct yourself with *positive* words. Do *not* use words that are going to create more negative reinforcement! That would only defeat your purpose. For example, don't say something like, "Smith, you stupid idiot! You don't even have the brains of a chicken egg!" Such words can be detrimental to your self-esteem and, therefore, your ability to succeed.

Instead say something like, "Smith, you sure used poor judgment in that situation. You knew better than that. You're intelligent, but you got lax and allowed yourself to behave like a jerk. But you aren't a jerk. You're a winner, and I want you to *behave* like one! Do you hear me, Smith? Behave like the champion you really are!"

Put a lot of emotion into your words so you *really* understand what you're saying at a deep level. Raise your voice at yourself and honestly get with the program! You are your own coach, encouraging yourself to increase your performance, pointing out your potential to win. You are also encouraging yourself to straighten yourself out and get with the program so you can do better the next time.

There are an infinite number of encouraging scenarios, depending on the situation and your personality. In a few moments, you will read several scenarios complete with accompanying *SCOREing* Approaches as general guidelines, and you can take it from there.

When do you need to straighten yourself out? As soon as practical after you make a mistake. It may be immediately, later that day, or even the next day, depending on the situation. But be sure to do it while the mistake is still fresh in your mind. Too much delay is detrimental. It would tell your subconscious that you are tolerant of your mistakes and excuse making rather than correcting them and moving on—thus reinforcing an unacceptable behavior.

Where would you do it? You definitely want to be alone when you straighten yourself out. The reasons for this are obvious. Personally, I have three favorite places: in the shower, in the bathroom in front of the mirror, and in the car.

The shower is my favorite place because there I am relaxed and alone. The door is closed, and I can think very clearly when I am being sprinkled with soothing warm water. There I can talk out loud vigorously without disturbing my wife.

In front of a mirror is also an excellent place for straightening yourself out. In fact, it is an excellent place to *SCORE*—for any purpose. Look yourself in the eye and really take yourself to task. It's actually kind of fun and can bring excellent results.

I *SCORE* in my car when I don't want to wait until I get home to take a shower or look into the mirror. I often use the car to address any minor mistakes I may have made in my office. For example, I made an error in writing a document that caused me to rework it and I was embarrassed the next day. I straightened myself out on this while driving home. It was fresh on my mind, and this enabled me do deal with it as effectively as possible.

Encourage yourself simply by recognizing your *behavior*—how you acted—instead of calling yourself names, labeling yourself, and hurting your self-esteem. When you give yourself instructions for how you want to behave in the future, do so in positive terms. If you tell yourself *not* to do something, your subconscious doesn't hear the not—it only hears the something! *Your mind cannot focus on the opposite of an idea.* For example, if someone tells you to not think about the pink elephant, what do you do? Think of the pink elephant! You just can't get it out of your mind, no matter how hard you may try.

Here are three sample scenarios and approaches to give you some ideas on how to effectively *SCORE* to straighten yourself out after making a mistake:

In the first scenario, you have overslept and are driving to work—running a few minutes behind your usual schedule. A traffic light turns red just as you reach the intersection. You decide to proceed through anyway so you can make up for some lost time—even though you could have easily stopped. A car sitting at the intersection makes a "jack rabbit" start the instant his light turns green. You collide in the middle of the intersection. Fortunately, there are no injuries. But several thousand dollars damage was done to both cars, tempers flared, and a lot of time was wasted. You made a mistake by exercising poor judgment.

SCOREing Approach #1—*Driving Safely*

Later that day, in a quiet place where you are alone, you encouraged yourself. Your dialogue might have gone something like this, using as much emotion as you can muster:

First, verbally review your mistake—"I messed up royally today! I broke the law and caused a collision because I was in a hurry. There's no excuse for being in a hurry and jeopardizing my safety and that of others. I had just overslept, that was all.

"I was lucky this time. No one was injured, and my insurance will take care of all but the deductible."

Now verbally correct yourself—"I behaved in a totally irresponsible manner. That is not the way I want to be and it's certainly not my usual behavior. I wasn't as clear headed as I could have been, and there is no excuse for that. No one forced me to oversleep.

"I am totally responsible for my actions, and I am disappointed that I let myself down in this situation. I have no right to endanger anyone's life, and yet that is exactly what I did. I acted in a completely unacceptable manner." (*Here you really raise your voice.*)

"I SAID, I ACTED IN A COMPLETELY UNACCEPTABLE MANNER! THERE'S NO EXCUSE!

"I caused another person to be inconvenienced and their property to be damaged. I HAVE ABSOLUTELY NO RIGHT TO DO THAT! I AM ASHAMED OF MY BEHAVIOR. I AM TRULY SORRY FOR MY THOUGHTLESS ACTIONS."

Now verbally define what you're going to do about it—"I vow to myself to always act responsibly. I SAID, I WILL ALWAYS ACT RESPONSIBLY—ALWAYS—WHATEVER IT TAKES! I am a considerate, responsible person by nature, but this time I really exercised poor judgment. I don't want to ever make a mistake like that again. I will strive to be even more alert, more caring, and more responsible in all my actions in the future.

"I now vow to keep all my priorities straight—*always*. My first priority is to always be respectful of other people's lives and property. There is no excuse for jeopardizing either, and I shall behave in a responsible manner from now on.

"I forgive myself for my thoughtless behavior, and put it behind me. I am resolved to do better every day and eliminate irresponsible behavior from my life."

This scenario gives you an idea of how to encourage yourself when you make a mistake that created or could have created serious consequences. Within this concept you can develop your own approach and use words you are comfortable with.

Whenever you use a mirror during a *SCOREing* session, you might want to address your image by name instead of just saying "I." Say something like, "Smith, you really messed up royally today!" Using a "second party" approach like that can also be very effective in helping you get the results you want. Performing a *SCOREing* session like this programs your subconscious mind (your obedient servant) to:

1. Acknowledge your behavior truthfully.
2. Cleanse yourself of negative thinking.
3. Institute and reinforce new, positive thinking to guide your future behavior.

You have recognized the behavior you no longer want to continue, and have given your subconscious mind clear instructions concerning what you want your future behavior to be.

—End of *SCOREing* Approach #1

Most of us like to clown around once in a while. When done in good taste and with sensitivity, it can be fun and pleasant.

However, what about those times when clowning around is done in poor taste and is insensitive? An innocent person is likely to be embarrassed and feel hurt. When it is your clowning that caused the hurt feelings, how do you handle it?

In the second scenario, I address such a situation. I have arbitrarily chosen a male to do the clowning and a male to be the recipient of it. The scenario is valid, however, regardless of who says what to whom.

A coworker is escorting a new employee around the department to introduce him. The new employee is neat, clean, and dressed in a freshly pressed suit with a white shirt and tie. His suit, frankly, has seen its better days and is obviously a little outdated.

When he's introduced to you, you say, "Glad to meet you. Welcome to the department. In case no one warned you, I am the department clown."

He smiles, shakes your hand and says, "I'm glad to be part of this department, clown and all. Nice to meet you."

You deliberately look him up and down, and say, "I hope your starting salary is enough so you can buy a new suit."

Then you grin as if you had just spoken the funniest line ever written. Only no one else is smiling. The new employee's face becomes flushed and somber. The coworker quickly rushes him away and changes the subject in an attempt to soften the situation. You stand there alone. Your grin disappears as you realize you have behaved like the south end of a north-bound horse. So, what do you do now? You cannot undo what you said. Yet, you know you need to remedy the situation you created by being inconsiderate.

SCOREing Approach #2—*Apologizing for Bad Humor*

First, as soon as you can, head directly to a place where you'll be alone. Tell yourself out loud that you behaved like the south end of a north-bound horse, that you are sorry, and that you will never do it again.

Second, say, "(The man's name), this is (your name). I am truly sorry for my crude, insensitive remark. I could have had the compassion to realize you may have been having a difficult time, and this job may be offering you a chance to improve your situation. I now realize that I put you down, and I had no right to do so. I just thought I was being funny, but I wasn't. Sometimes I get carried away with what I think is humorous. I didn't intend to be rude to you. I am truly sorry. Please forgive me."

Third, you may want to go to a store and buy a suitable greeting card or "welcome" gift such as an inexpensive desk pen and pencil set, or perhaps a small box of chocolates. If at all possible, do this the same day, perhaps on your lunch hour. If you can't go right away, do it before coming to work the next day. This is an absolute step. *SCOREing* by itself does not get you off the hook in all situations. Here is a case where you need to augment your *SCOREing* with concrete corrective action.

Fourth, now it's time to go directly to the person so you can apologize as soon as possible after your inappropriate behavior. If you are able to get the welcome card or gift right away, great. Otherwise, apologize and give it to him or her later. You offended that person and you need to make amends.

Fifth, that evening, make some time to *SCORE* another encouragement session with yourself, using the first and second steps of this approach. During this session, be sure to apologize to the new employee again. And be sure to forgive yourself as well. Resolve to "grow up" and communicate with your coworkers and associates in a complimentary way, rather than clowning around and perhaps offending someone. Repeat this *SCOREing* session with yourself for two more nights, then move on from it.

— End of *SCOREing* Approach #2

The first and second scenarios illustrate that *SCOREing* alone is sometimes not enough, particularly if you've done some serious damage to a relationship or somebody else's property. In the first scenario, you would also have had to make financial restitution if your insurance had not covered it. (You could have also apologized to the driver with whom you collided.) As it is, you had to pay your deductible, and probably had to appear in traffic court and pay court costs as well as a fine. In addition to all that, your insurance rates most likely increased. Ouch!

Mistakes can be expensive, which is one of the reasons *SCOREing* is such an invaluable tool. It enables you to change your thinking and acting, and thereby increase your awareness so you can eliminate or, at least, greatly reduce the number and severity of your mistakes.

Now before we leave the second scenario, here's something else for you to consider. In addition to apologizing face to face, I had also twice directed the "clown" to apologize during a *SCOREing* session when he was all alone. There are two reasons for this: First, this person needs to condition his subconscious so he can be more sensitive and caring in the future. Second, talking out loud to someone who is not physically present is a powerful mechanism that can help you heal the relationship. It's a great habit to get into.

In the third scenario, which follows, we have a situation where *SCOREing,* alone, would completely atone for an act of rudeness and unkindness. This is an actual situation that happened to me on a subway train in New York City. The people who did it to me didn't use *SCOREing* or any other sort of restitution. I will share what they *could* have done by using the *SCOREing* approach.

In this scenario, I was an out-of-towner on business. My hotel was in uptown Manhattan while my business appointment was downtown. I decided to take the subway because it is the fastest and least expensive way to get around the city. When I boarded the subway, my car was only about half full. I picked out a seat and sat down. But after a couple more stops, the car was completely jammed. All the seats were filled and people were standing in every available space, firmly hanging onto straps and poles.

A woman, who was visibly quite pregnant and carrying a package, boarded the car and stood hanging onto a strap about a half-car away from me. None of the men sitting near her offered her a seat. Being a born-and-raised-polite mid-westerner, I could not tolerate seeing a pregnant woman stand while I sat. I stood up, caught her eye and said, "Ma'am, you may have my seat."

I will never forget what happened next. She glared at me, then sneered and said in a voice as cold and hard as tempered steel, "What are you, some kind of freak?" Then she actually turned her back to me, continuing to stand there holding onto the strap!

At that moment, while I was still half standing, preparing to give her my seat, a scruffy young man, who was with a group of his equally disheveled friends, forced himself between me and my seat and claimed it for his own! His tough-looking friends just roared with laughter. They thought it was all so very funny.

My Irish instinct was to have a confrontation with the young man but, fortunately, my better judgment prevailed. In that environment, who knows what could have happened? So I rode on to my stop in silence, burning with anger over the extreme rudeness of the woman and the young men.

SCOREing Approach #3—*Apologizing for Rude Behavior*

I related the incident to the president of the company with whom I had my business appointment. He was a big city dweller who had grown up in the streets.

"That's just the way some people are here," he said. "You midwesterners are naïve."

What had been anger now turned to empathy for these people who had allowed themselves to become so hardened and insensitive in their attitudes. I instantly harbored no negative feelings toward them. They had created a difficult situation for themselves that I had no intention of adding to with retaliatory feelings. In those days, the *SCOREing* concept had not yet been developed. But even if it had, that woman and young man would probably not have had the awareness or sensitivity to use it.

Let's hypothesize what *SCOREing* approach they might have used. They couldn't have sent me a note saying they were sorry for their conduct because they didn't know my name or where I lived. However, they could have corrected themselves for their behavior. They could also have said a simple, "Sorry about that," and resolved to change their behavior. They could have done this with the *SCOREing* approaches described in this chapter, had they known about them, and it would have made a difference for the better. But obviously they didn't. They were probably just imitating someone else and the discourtesies they had witnessed, perhaps at home or in other places.

—End of *SCOREing* Approach #3

The innumerable people who could have at least made an effort to make up for their poor behavior *but didn't* are the ones who degenerate into creating unsuccessful and unhappy lives for themselves and their families. And who do they generally blame? Other people, of course.

The people who could have apologized *and do* are the ones who lift themselves to new heights of happiness and success. For one thing, they're not carrying around the excess baggage of old, unresolved grievances.

SCOREing is one practice that can make the difference between acceptable and unacceptable behavior, between success and failure, between truly living and merely existing. What we are really talking about here is creating positive energy and canceling out the negative by implementing certain approaches using the simple yet effective process of *SCOREing*. Think about it. Just get busy with your mouth and start *SCOREing* your way to a better life.

"The world has a way of giving what is demanded of it. If you are frightened and look for failure and poverty, you will get them, no matter how hard you may try to succeed. Lack of faith in yourself, in what life will do for you, cuts you off from the good things of the world. Expect victory and you make victory. Nowhere is this truer than in business, that is, when bravery and faith bring both material and spiritual rewards."

—Preston Bradley

"*Fear can thwart success in any endeavor, but only if we allow it to do so. It can cripple our potential and keep us from reaching for our dreams and goals. Fortunately, SCOREing can be used to overcome any fear we may have.*"

—Bill Wayne

-3-

Are You a Fraidy Cat?
SCOREing to Overcome Fear

"A hero is no braver than an ordinary man,
but he is brave five minutes longer."
—Ralph Waldo Emerson—

One spring, my wife and I went on a 73-day motor-home trip through the southern United States. Upon reaching a state campground near Waurika, Oklahoma, we pulled in for the night. It was a beautiful place, and we were the only ones there.

"I wonder why no one else is here?" my wife asked as she tuned in a local radio station on our radio.

As if on cue, the announcer gave his station's call letters and said, "Welcome to Waurika, Oklahoma, the rattlesnake capital of the world. There are more rattlesnakes here per square mile than anywhere else in the world."

My blood ran cold. Yet I was too tired to continue driving to get further away, and we both needed to rest. But I wasn't about to go outside. Fortunately, our motor home is completely equipped, so there was no need to go outside and, believe me, we didn't!

There may not have been a snake of any kind within a mile, but I didn't intend to find out. The radio announcer's greeting triggered the only fear I have ever had—a fear of snakes. So I chose to remain captive in my motor home, paralyzed by a fear that may not have even had any real basis in fact. Frankly, I was a little ashamed of my behavior, but I let fear dominate me.

Back then, I had been using *SCOREing* only for a limited number of purposes—memory improvement, success statements, or job interview preparation. I hadn't yet discovered the enormous power of *SCOREing* for virtually any situation. It never occurred to me to use *SCOREing* to overcome my fear of snakes, so I stayed imprisoned, gripped by a feeling of helplessness. Intellectually, I knew I wasn't behaving rationally. But fear is a powerful emotion, and I had allowed it to overpower my rational reasoning. Fear can thwart success in any endeavor by crippling our potential and keeping us from reaching for our dreams and goals, but only if we allow it to do so.

In the ensuing years, I had developed my expertise in *SCOREing* for a wide range of situations. But I had not yet done any work on fear control through *SCOREing*. There was no need to. I had never knowingly had another potential encounter with a snake, as I shared, and I had no fears other than that of snakes. Then one day, we planned a week-long camping trip into the Rocky Mountains of Colorado.

Snakes! The image jumped into my mind and the fear threatened to overwhelm me. The mountains were a haven for all sorts of snakes and other wildlife, but only the snakes concerned me. For example, if I were to meet a bear face to face, it wouldn't scare me. I would be concerned, of course, and would quickly get out of its way, but I would remain calm and in control. At the mere mention of snakes, though, that control became history! And I just knew I had to change this. Enough was enough, and I was determined to wipe out my fear of snakes right then and there. My thoughts immediately turned to *SCOREing*. After all, I had witnessed, firsthand, what a powerful tool *SCOREing* had been for me in a vast array of circumstances. I knew *SCOREing* was the answer.

SCOREing Approach #4—*Overcoming Fear*
The night before we were to leave on our Rocky Mountain camping trip, I settled into a tubful of warm water and had a serious

SCOREing session with myself concerning my fear of snakes. It went something like this:

"Bill, you are intelligent and reasonable. You are also a logical thinker. So why do you think so illogically when it comes to snakes?"

"I don't know."

"Has a snake ever hurt you?"

"No."

"You know that snakes play an important role in the balance of nature, don't you?"

"Yes, I know that."

"You can walk faster than a snake can slither, so, even if it wanted to, it couldn't catch you. You also have the power to kill them, and you can easily outsmart them.

"In fact, snakes can't do much at all lay hang around and eat bugs and rodents. They are doing you a favor. They are your friends because they help control pests.

"They don't even like to be around people and avoid us whenever possible. If you don't like being around them, for goodness sake, stay off their turf!"

I continued in that vein for awhile. Then I told myself that the next time I saw a snake, I wouldn't be afraid. Instead, I'd be calm and in control, and would react no differently than if I had encountered any other wild creature. I reinforced these *SCOREing* commands several more times. My total bathtub *SCOREing* session lasted no more than 30 minutes.

—End of *SCOREing* Approach #4

We had been set up in camp for just a couple of hours when, lo and behold, I saw a snake! I was standing relaxed, legs wide apart, taking in the majesty of the mountains, the freshness of the pine trees, and the rush of the whitewater next to our campsite. I glanced down and saw a three-foot gopher snake slithering between my legs as if it were passing under the Arc de Triumphe going someplace important.

I wasn't afraid. I saw the snake for what it was—just another wild creature doing the best it could to get along in the world.

Nearby was a small branch, about the thickness of my little finger, three or four feet long. I picked it up to help me deal with the snake. I carefully slid the branch midway under its belly so as not to hurt or frighten it. As I gently picked it up with the stick, I even spoke out loud to it, "I am going to move you to a safer place, little buddy. You could get injured if you stay here."

I walked about a hundred feet away, across a dirt road and onto the slope of a hill, where I carefully lowered the snake into the grass. It quickly slithered away. Again, I spoke out loud, "I'll make you a deal. You stay here and I'll stay at my campsite."

The fear was gone. I felt really good about myself. I handled the situation calmly and appropriately. I did not harm the snake, nor did it harm me. At no time was I even a little bit anxious or nervous. I saw the snake from an entirely different perspective than I ever had seen snakes before.

I view my encounter with the snake, which happened soon after my *SCOREing* session, as being a test to show me that *SCOREing* truly works. Since then, I have not had any other encounters with snakes and probably never will again. Fear is like that. Once you face it, deal with it, and conquer it, it is gone forever. It will never bother or deter you again!

Here's an example of a situation many people face while building a home-based business, outside of their jobs, to increase their income. Perhaps they desire to associate with other like-minded, positive-thinking people so they can build an organization with them. However, even though many of those people could have a fairly extensive list of contacts, some of those contacts may already be very successful. This might cause some trepidation about approaching people like doctors or other highly esteemed professionals, out of the fear of being rejected. If so, one or more good *SCOREing* sessions can help. So, if you ever find yourself in this situation, or know someone who is, here's how it could go:

SCOREing Approach #5—*Sharing an Opportunity*
Talking to yourself in your bathroom mirror, you say:
"Are you afraid of contacting your doctor and other successful people you know with whom you could share your opportunity?"
"Yes."

"Do you realize that those people may be wealthy but not have other things that are important to them?"

"Yes."

"Take your doctor for instance. He's actually commented to you that he'd love to be able to retire early so he can travel to third-world countries and donate his medical services, didn't he?"

"Yes."

"Isn't the opportunity you have to share the kind of thing that could give him the time and income he needs so he can quit his practice?"

"Yes."

"Well, then go ahead and give him a call. What's the worst thing that could happen—he says he's not interested, right?"

"True."

"Can you accept that possibility and think 'next' and then call the next person on your list?"

"Sure, I can do that!"

"Well, (say your name), get off your stubbornness and start making calls so you can share your wonderful opportunity with others who will appreciate it. What are you waiting for? The time is now."

—End of *SCOREing* Approach #5

No matter what fear you may have, you can use *SCOREing* to help you understand and rid yourself of it. Write your own *SCOREing* script. If need be, ask for help from a leader or mentor with whom you may be working.

Not all fears may disappear as quickly and easily as mine did. Some fears might require repeated *SCOREing* sessions over a period of time. Some fears could be so deeply ingrained that professional help may be required, but *SCOREing* can help accelerate the process.

People let fear imprison them and hold them hostage. *SCOREing* frees people. Get free of fear. Start *SCOREing* today and continue doing it until the fear is overcome. Make it happen!

"**S**COREing really works! It helps you clearly think through what you want to accomplish and how you need to go about doing it. It gives you the added boost of confidence you need to get it done."

—Bill Wayne

-4-

Psst... Have I Got a Deal for You!
SCOREing to Make a Purchase

"Our plans miscarry because they have no aim. When a man does not know what harbor he is making for, no wind is the right wind."
—Seneca—

This chapter can apply to any major purchase you may be considering. It is tailored toward buying a motor vehicle because this can be the most precarious buying experience many of us will ever have, especially if we're not prepared. After all, the odds are usually stacked in favor of the dealer. If you walk into a showroom without being prepared, you may have about as much of a chance of getting a good deal as when you drop a silver dollar into a slot machine!

Think about it. You may purchase a vehicle perhaps once every four years or so and most likely less often than that. But the salesperson's goal is to sell vehicles every day, no matter what. Which of you has the most experience in the automobile sales business, you or the salesperson? The salesperson, of course. So if that person is desperate to meet a quota, or doesn't care about you or have integrity, your chances of getting a less-than-optimum deal are quite good.

In all fairness, most vehicle dealers have cleaned up their act in recent years and strive to be reputable. But remember, they are in business to earn as much money as they can, and you are one of their potential sources.   Nevertheless, it is still a buyer-beware market. Therefore, we need all the assistance we can get when buying a vehicle. Fortunately, *SCOREing* can be a significant help.

Even though I had been using *SCOREing* many years for other purposes, until a decade or so ago I hadn't used it for purchasing an automobile. But then one day, it occurred to me that *SCOREing* could be used for buying a car, or making any other major purchase for that matter. It took two previous challenging experiences with auto dealers to shake me into action, before I could crystallize the idea of using *SCOREing* to buy a car. I'll tell you about them to give you a good understanding of how *SCOREing* Approach #6 for buying a vehicle was developed.

Early one year, I thought it might be a good idea to buy my wife a new car and let her old one just be a backup. There was a car she liked, so we went into the dealership nearest our home. A salesman appeared and quickly wrote some figures on a piece of paper, and we began dickering. Within minutes he decreased the asking price until our payments would be $500 a month for 60 months with a $10,000 downpayment. It was an excellent deal on a new convertible, fully loaded with all the extras, that carried a sticker price of $40,000. He never argued with us. It was the easiest deal we had ever made.

He said, "I'll take this paper back to the sales assistant to be written into a formal contract. It should be ready in about 15 minutes." He then disappeared.

All the while, though, something kept gnawing at me. I didn't know what was bothering me about this transaction, but something just didn't seem right. I felt the salesman wasn't being totally honest with me. So I spoke my thoughts out loud matter-of-factly to my wife. In retrospect, I now realize that I was actually *SCOREing*.

"Something isn't quite right," I said. "What do I need to know? What questions do I need to ask? What am I overlooking? What isn't the salesman telling us?"

I immediately understood that I needed to read the contract very carefully before signing it. A split second after I got that idea, my wife said to me, "You had better check the contract carefully. I don't feel right about this either."

The salesman reappeared, completed contract in hand, with a Cheshire-cat grin plastered on his face. He had the contract folded to the last page—the signature page.

"Just sign here, and you can drive your beautiful new convertible away within a few short minutes," he said, tapping his finger by the signature line while thrusting a ballpoint pen at me with his other hand.

"I am going to read it first," I said.

"No need to," he said. "It is exactly as we agreed. I'll tell you what it says to save you time."

He picked up the contract, flipped quickly to the first page, and pointed to two entries as he spoke. "See, five hundred a month and ten thousand down, just as we discussed." He quickly flipped back to the signature page. "The rest is just the standard mumbo jumbo about warranties and responsibilities."

I laid the pen aside and picked up the contract. "I will read it first," I said.

The Cheshire-cat grin disappeared. He walked off mumbling that he would be back when I finished.

Within a few seconds, I discovered the discrepancy. He had written in 72 months on the contract, instead of 60, as the term of the loan. That would increase my cost by $9,000! No wonder he had not argued about the deal. He had deceitfully planned to increase the profit of the contract.

When he returned, I confronted him. He said we had agreed on 72 months. I asked him to get the paper he had originally written. He immediately told me that he had thrown it away.

"How difficult is it for you to get it from the wastebasket?" I asked determinedly. I was now certain that the 72 months was not an inadvertent typographical error.

He made a facial contortion, expressing his displeasure. "I'll see if I can find it."

When he did not return within five minutes, my wife and I got up and walked out of the showroom. He must have been watching because he came running after us.

"The wastebasket was emptied into the dumpster and had already been picked up and hauled away before I could get it. If you come back in, I am sure we can work out a deal."

"Don't insult our intelligence," I snapped. "You lied, and you tried to cheat us. We will never ever return to this dealership again."

We drove away. My wife was so angry that she said she didn't want a new car for a while. Although I didn't recognize it at the time, the seeds for *SCOREing* to buy a car had been sown in my mind.

It was nearly two more years before we went to buy again. This second experience watered and nurtured the seeds, causing them to sprout. It was near the end of the year, and the new models were out. I noticed my wife had been looking at new car ads in the magazines, so I suggested she might want to shop for one.

"I know what I want," she said. "A Cadillac Seville STS because it has class without being a snob about it."

"Then we will go out this coming Saturday to look," I responded.

We had decided that through a creative financial option, we'd pay cash for the car because we figured (correctly so) that we could get a better deal for cash up-front. We also knew we could save on expensive interest charges. (As an aside, these are valuable practices for wealth-building. Most people just blindly follow what the dealerships offer them, rather than carefully thinking it through.)

We had a modest savings account at our credit union, but we didn't want to deplete it. So we took $50,000 of the savings and put it in a Certificate of Deposit (CD). We put the CD up for collateral at the credit union. The credit union then loaned us $50,000 at just one percentage point over the interest rate they were paying us on the CD. They also arranged our loan repayment so we didn't have to pay higher monthly payments than we wanted to. It was a really good deal for us—a healthy $50,000 loan at a 1 percent cost and our original $50,000 was still ours in a CD. We put the $50,000 into our checking account, which also paid us interest—we were ready to go on our car shopping adventure.

Let me digress for a moment to tell you something about my wife because it is germane to the story. She is Chinese. The Chinese in general—and my wife in particular—are second to none when it comes to bartering. They are experts in the art of dealing, and she is the personification of that art.

Every day, for the five days until Saturday, she told and re-told me her 10-step plan in detail. It went something like this:

SCOREing Approach #6—*Buying a Vehicle*

1. I am going to lay down the ground rules with the salesperson immediately. If he or she doesn't play by my rules, I'm going to walk out and I will not return—no matter what.
2. Colors that are totally unacceptable to me are black, burgundy, green, and white.
3. I will not accept the small "emergency" spare tire that cars come with today. It must be a full-size spare that exactly matches the ones on the car, and there must be no extra charge for it.
4. I want the top-of-the-line AM-FM stereo radio, and both a cassette player and a 12-CD changer.
5. I must have an automatic transmission, air conditioning, moon roof, rain sensor, heated seats, chrome wheels, the works—she went on to list almost every option possible.
6. I will take my checkbook and write out a check for a 100 percent cash deal. No dealer financing.
7. I will not dicker. The salesperson will have one chance to quote me his or her best price. If it is higher than I am willing to pay, I will walk out and not buy.
8. I will not tolerate the salesperson showing me any car other than one that meets the specifications I have told him or her.
9. I will not tolerate the salesperson having to run back and forth to the sales manager to shave a few dollars off the price.
10. The price the salesperson quotes me must be one total price that includes all taxes, dealer add-ons, and so forth. If he or she tries to add any amount onto the quoted price after we make the deal, I will walk out and not buy. I want the total drive-it-off-the-lot price, and I will write out a check for the total amount right then and there.

—End of *SCOREing* Approach #6

At the time, of course, neither of us realized she was doing a perfect *SCOREing* routine! She was merely doing what her innate sense of business craftsmanship told her to do. At that time, I had approached *SCOREing* as something one must do alone. The thought that this was also *SCOREing* never even entered my mind.

When we arrived at the dealership that Saturday, not surprisingly, a salesman immediately latched onto us, like a bulldog on a mailman's leg. My wife told him, "I came to buy a car. I have some ironclad ground rules, and if you are really interested in selling, listen carefully." She then repeated, from memory, all of the points she had reiterated out loud to me many times during the preceding five days.

The salesman smiled and said, "No problem." He then showed her three Sevilles—blue, gray, and tan—that met her specifications. She liked the blue one, and pointed out that it didn't have a full-size spare tire.

"We can get you one next week," the salesman said.

"You weren't paying attention when I laid down the rules. I drive it off the lot today exactly how I want it, or I don't buy it at all. Period!"

The salesman sort of winced and walked over to speak to another man. Then he returned to us. The other man scurried off, and within 15 minutes was back with a matching full-size spare tire, which he put into the trunk of the car.

"Now what is your lowest price? Remember you have just one shot. No dickering."

The sticker price was over $52,000. The salesman said the most he could come down on his own was to $50,000 but that the sales manager could authorize more. He excused himself to go talk to the sales manager and returned with a price of $49,000.

"You *can't* be serious!" my wife scolded. "You aren't even *close* to a reasonable price. Thanks for your time. Goodbye." She turned abruptly to leave and bumped into a man who had just walked into the showroom.

"Is there a problem?" the man asked.

"Not really. I am going to buy a car today, but not here. The sales manager doesn't want to sell me that car over there." She pointed to the blue Seville.

"What price did the sales manager quote?"

My wife told him, "$49,000."

The man introduced himself and added, "I own this dealership. Will you give me one chance to sell you that car?"

"You have 15 minutes. Here are the ground rules." She went over them. "Your time starts now." She looked at her watch.

"I'll tell you what," the owner said. "You write on a piece of paper the most you are willing to pay. I'll write on another piece of paper the least I am willing to sell the car for—our bottom line. Then we'll play show and tell. If my figure matches yours or is lower than yours, you write me out a check for my figure right now and the car is yours. If my figure is higher than yours, you walk out and don't buy. No hassles. Okay?"

"We are talking about total price, right?" my wife asked. "No add-on taxes or anything else?"

"Right."

"You've got a deal!"

They each wrote on a paper and then played showdown. My wife had written $45,000. He had written $44,200. My wife wrote a check for $44,200 immediately and we drove off in her $52,000+ car. She had captured nearly an $8,000 savings with her take-charge attitude!

I thought about those two car-shopping experiences a lot over the following three years or so, and I finally concluded that *SCOREing* was at work in both cases. I also concluded that you don't always have to be alone when talking to yourself to have a valid *SCOREing* session. You can talk to yourself as if you're talking to someone else. My wife was insightful enough to know that, and she knew it was effective.

I decided to put it to the test personally to either validate or invalidate my *SCOREing* theory. My car was nearly eight years old and needed about $5,000 in repairs if I were to keep it much longer. Putting more money into it didn't seem like a financially sound idea, so I opted to buy myself a new vehicle. (For some, it's wiser to just repair the original vehicle or buy a three-to-four-year-old used vehicle.)

It was June. I wanted a Jeep Grand Cherokee. I followed the exact pattern my wife had established over three years before. Following *SCOREing* Approach #6, I *SCORED* to myself when alone as well as in her presence. I established my ground rules script just as she had done.

I went to the dealership and quickly spotted the exact car I wanted—except it had an emergency spare tire instead of a regular full-size one. The sticker price was $39,000. I stuck to my programmed script. *Deja Vu!* In less than two hours after walking in, I drove my Jeep out, with a full-size matching spare tire, for $32,000— a $7,000 savings!

Yes, *SCOREing* really works! It helps you clearly think through what you want to accomplish and how you need to go about it. It gives you the added boost of confidence you need to get it done.

I told a friend in St. Paul, Minnesota, about how I *SCORED* my way to purchasing the Jeep. She excitedly wrote to share with me that she also used the *SCOREing* approach for buying a new car—on *her* terms. She thanked me for my help.

If you are going to buy a vehicle, whether new or used, follow *SCOREing* Approach #6, creating your own script. Chances are excellent you will get what you want at the price you want to pay. The great thing is, you can modify this procedure for virtually any major purchase.

"**S**coring is always simple. You just meet the situation head-on by talking it over out loud with yourself. Ask simple, direct questions and give simple, direct answers—and you will lead yours to exactly where you want to be."

—Bill Wayne

"*Hit or miss just won't cut it— you need to be dedicated and relentless in your quest to make the change.*"

—Bill Wayne

-5-

Kicking Bad Health Habits and Creating Good Ones
SCOREing for Good Health Habits

> *"The nature of men is always the same; it is their habits that separate them."*
> —Confucius—

Nearly everyone has some sort of bad health habit. It might be chewing fingernails, nervous eye blinking, cracking knuckles, grinding teeth, eating unhealthy foods, overeating or undereating, smoking or chewing tobacco, or something else. Most people with such habits would like to get rid of them and replace them with good habits.

SCOREing can empower you to eliminate any bad health habits you may have. In this chapter, you will learn approaches to deal with two of the most challenging, and probably most widespread, bad habits: poor diet and smoking. These two *SCOREing* approaches can serve as models for you to tackle any bad habit and get rid of it. You would only need to modify the approaches to fit your situation. I am confident these two approaches will fit many of you perfectly.

—Part A—
Think Healthy
SCOREing a Good Diet

Current fad dictates that if you are heftier than a broom handle, you need to lose weight. Magazines, television, newspapers, the Internet, radio, and junk mail bombard you with products the advertisers feel you need to purchase—to have a thinner, healthier body and a more glamorous life.

I personally do not subscribe to the be-skinny fanaticism. I am more interested in a person's heart, mind, and character than in their physical dimensions. However, this chapter is not a discussion of my philosophy so I will stick to the facts. We live in a thin-is-better society. I do agree, however, that we all need to live a healthy lifestyle. And, sometimes, being healthier means one needs to lose a few pounds.

There are probably as many methods to lose weight as there are overweight people. So I will give you one more aid to weight reduction for your consideration—*SCOREing*. That's right, you can "talk" your weight off. It is slower than diet pills, but certainly safer. And it is faster than doing nothing! But, before we go any further, I feel it's important for me to make several things clear:

1. I am not a medical doctor, and this chapter is not intended to be medical advice.
2. If you decide you want to lose weight, do so only under the direction of your doctor.
3. Use the *SCOREing* Approach in *Part A* only to augment your medically approved eating plan. It is *not* a replacement for any medical advice.

SCOREing your weight off works best when used in conjunction with a sensible eating plan. And it works faster than just following that plan without *SCOREing*. In showing you how to lose weight via

SCOREing, I will employ a sample eating plan to give you the idea of combining such a plan with *SCOREing.* The eating plan I use here is for illustration purposes only, and I do not mean to imply that it is the best one for you. It is only an example.

Selecting a proper eating plan is a serious matter. *Be sure to consult your healthcare professional* and use your own good sense in making the selection. I am not a nutritional expert nor a healthcare professional. I only offer guidance in teaching how to use *SCOREing* in conjunction with your own program to make it even more successful.

The *SCOREing* approach will be to say your eating plan out loud before each meal, along with some supportive statements. Then after each meal, say some supportive statements, again, out loud. Here's how it can work, for example, in a sample eating plan that worked well for me follows as an example:

—*Breakfast*—
Small serving of protein (2 - 3 ounces)
Small serving of fruit or juice (4 ounces)
One piece of unbuttered toast
At least 2 glasses of water

—*Lunch*—
Small serving of protein (3 - 4 ounces)
Small serving of fresh fruit or vegetable
At least 2 glasses of water

—*Dinner*—
Small serving of protein (4 - 5 ounces)
Small salad with light dressing
Half cup of cooked vegetable served without butter
At least 2 glasses of water
No gravies or sauces

There are good reasons for using *SCOREing* in conjunction with your eating plan. First, most people fail in their eating plans because they don't stick to them faithfully. *SCOREing* is a self-disciplining mechanism that helps you to develop the tendency to stick with your program. Second, as you know by now from the preceding chapters,

SCOREing is a powerful reinforcement mechanism for achieving any goal. The eating plan/*SCOREing* program gives you a triple whammy, so to speak.

1. You tell yourself out loud what you are going to eat and why. This sets your mind up to be more receptive to following your eating plan.
2. Eat the planned meal you have just described. This satisfies your mind's goal-seeking quest, and also reinforces your *SCOREing* and your commitment.
3. Finally, tell yourself out loud what you have just done and why you have done it. This is powerful reinforcement for the first two steps.

In combination, these three steps can help you eliminate any unhealthy eating tendencies you may have and replace them with healthy habits—effectively, and in a wholesome, supportive manner. But by about now, you may be wondering how you are going to read your *SCOREing* routine before and after meals, since you often eat in the presence of other people. That's really not a problem. Let's examine the three common eating scenarios: by yourself, with family, and outside of family.

Eating by yourself is not an issue. Just talk out loud to yourself as prescribed in *SCOREing* Approach #7A, presented below.

Eating with family members gives you two options. First, let them in on what you are doing so they can be supportive. It will be sort of a game, and they can help keep you on track. You just talk out loud to yourself at the table. They will not think anything of it because they are in on it. Second, if you do not want to use this option, then just go into another room for a few minutes, before and after the meal, to do your *SCOREing*. The bathroom is always a good choice because you know you can have privacy there.

When eating with non-family members (e.g., at a restaurant or at work), just go to the restroom and occupy one of the stalls for a few moments. You can talk softly (whisper) and no one will know. Just be sure to do the *SCOREing* every time as part of your eating program. Hit and miss just won't cut it—*you need to be dedicated and relentless in your quest to make the change.*

SCOREing Approach #7A—*Eating for Your Health*

Breakfast: Before eating, say this out loud: "In a few moments I am going to eat a healthy breakfast, (for example) consisting of a big glass of water, egg substitute on a piece of rye toast, and a four-ounce glass of orange juice. This breakfast will give me all the nourishment I need just now, and it will also fill me up. It will help me to lose excess weight in a sensible way, until I reach my desired weight. When I reach my desired weight, I will maintain that weight by continuing to eat sensibly."

Then eat your breakfast.

After breakfast, say out loud: "I have just eaten a nourishing breakfast that will help me lose excess weight. I only eat nutritious foods at meals. If I get hungry between meals, I drink water which is healthy and fills me up." (Remember, junk food is not an option.)

Lunch: Before eating, say out loud: "In a few moments I am going to eat a healthy lunch consisting of a big glass of water, a bowl of chicken soup, a side salad with low-fat dressing, and a small serving of applesauce (for example). This lunch will help me to lose excess pounds in a sensible way until I reach my desired weight. When I reach that weight, I will maintain it by continuing to eat sensibly."

Then eat your lunch.

After lunch, say out loud: "I have just eaten a nourishing lunch that will help me lose excess weight. I only eat food at meals. If I get hungry between meals I drink water, which is healthy and fills me up."

Dinner: Before eating, say out loud: "In a few moments I am going to eat a healthy dinner consisting of 4 ounces of baked chicken breast, a small lettuce and tomato salad with low-fat dressing, a half cup of sautéed zucchini, and a big glass of water (for example). This dinner will give me all the nourishment I need just now, and it will also fill me up. This dinner will help me to lose excess weight in a sensible way until I reach my desired weight. When I reach that weight, I will maintain it by continuing to eat sensibly."

Then eat your dinner.

After dinner, say out loud: "I have just eaten a nourishing dinner that will help me lose excess weight. I only eat nourishing food at meals. If I get hungry between meals I drink water, which is healthy and fills me up."

—End of *SCOREing* Approach #7A

Of course, you need to substitute the description of the food you are actually going to eat in place of the food I used in the *SCOREing* Approach #7A example.

That's all there is to it. When you follow this *SCOREing* approach faithfully every day, you will lose excess weight—guaranteed. Nothing could be simpler. You virtually talk off your excess weight!

—Part B—
No Smoking!
SCOREing to Quit Smoking

Nearly every smoker I know asserts that they want to stop smoking. "Someday I am going to quit." "I know it isn't good for me and I need to quit." "The doctor says my smoking is harmful to my baby, but…." And so it goes.

It's not that smokers aren't aware of all the negatives involved with smoking. They know that their breath smells like the inside of a chimney in a coal-fired power plant. Their clothes and their hair stink. Their smoke impregnates the clothing of other people, making them stink too. The rooms they smoke in stink. The inside of their vehicles stink.

More importantly, they know that the smoke not only harms their health but the health of others as well. They know that lungs were designed to take in clean air, yet they deliberately force their lungs to take in harmful air. It just doesn't make any sense now, does it?

It would take an extremely unaware person to believe that smoking wouldn't hurt him or her. Yet, generally speaking, smokers are intelligent, creative, and worthwhile contributors to society. So what's the problem? Why do intelligent people aggressively pursue an unintelligent, harmful activity? It seems as though they have done a "con job" on themselves. In an attempt to justify their habit, they have made themselves believe in the unbelievable.

If you stand on a railroad track in front of an oncoming train, and don't move, chances are you'll be killed. That's believable. Smokers, however, seem to have convinced themselves that the train will not hit them. Part of the challenge is that smoking tends to be addictive. The other part of it has to do with our mind's willingness to let us believe what we choose to believe regardless of whether the belief is valid or not.

There are a variety of products on the market that can supposedly help a person stop smoking. And while these products address the addictive aspect of smoking, they are not always effective. This means that the mentality of someone who smokes is the key that needs to be addressed. He or she needs to realize that there is too high a price to pay for the supposed short-term pleasure or stress reduction smoking may give. If smokers would change their mental state regarding smoking, many could become nonsmokers quickly—without necessarily needing the various products that deal with the addictive aspect. The more heavily addicted smokers would probably benefit from the stop-smoking products when used in conjunction with the self-induced mental change that can be accomplished through *SCOREing*.

I deliberately use the description "self-induced mental change" because the smoker is the only one who can make him or herself stop smoking. Anyone with a mind powerful enough to rationalize that an oncoming train will *not* hit them is also powerful enough to realize that it *will* hit them. This realization could well convince them to get out of the way. Smoking is a self-induced habit, and it has a self-induced solution. And becoming a *nonsmoker* is *also* a self-induced habit.

I have dealt with many smokers who said they wanted to quit. My experiences with those individuals validated everything I am writing in this chapter. Smokers are the *only* ones who can effectively stop themselves. Absolutely no one else can do it for them. There is no magic pill. Smokers need to reprogram their own minds to realistically see the oncoming train of cancer and emphysema.

This is where *SCOREing* enters the picture. If you are a smoker who really wants to kick the habit, *SCOREing* gives you a specific tool you can use to turn yourself into a nonsmoker. In a moment, you will read a suggested *SCOREing* re-programming procedure. You may use it as is, or you may want to alter the wording. In any case, you need to *SCORE* yourself daily as prescribed.

First of all, you need to be serious about wanting to stop smoking. If you are doing this because your spouse wants you to quit but you really don't want to, you have an excellent chance for failure. So think about this. Re-read this *Part B* a few times, then make up your own mind. To stop smoking, *you* must sincerely desire quitting the habit.

When you have honestly made up your mind, select a date to start. If possible, start the same day you made up your mind to do so, but be sure not to delay taking action longer than one week. If you are stalling for more than a week, you are not serious. Get a calendar you can mark up to keep track of your successful progress. Circle your starting day on the calendar and label it "Start." Now you are ready to proceed. Go forward with kicking the habit firmly in mind. Put it where you will easily see it every day.

SCOREing Approach #7B—*Quitting Smoking*

First Day: You will be allowed to continue smoking this first day only, but exercise your willpower to reduce the amount you smoke. When you get up in the morning, stand in front of your bathroom mirror. Look yourself in the eye, and say out loud to yourself the following words *three times*: "Today, (date), is the last day I will smoke tobacco in any form."

At day's end, while puffing on your final smoke, read the following out loud to yourself *three times*: "This is the last time I will smoke or use tobacco in any form. I am making a commitment to myself to become a nonsmoker from the moment I finish this smoke, and I always keep my commitments. When I awaken tomorrow morning I will be a confirmed nonsmoker."

After you finish that last smoke, immediately destroy whatever remaining tobacco products you have. Tear them up! Crush them! Throw them into the trash can, never to be retrieved. Then put an "X" through that day on your calendar to signify success. Now go to bed feeling good about your accomplishment.

Second Day: From this day on, throughout the rest of this *SCOREing* program, ask others not to smoke in your house, your vehicle, and your office or work area. Explain to them that it will help you achieve your goal to quit smoking and they will probably admire you and be happy to oblige. After you have completed the program, it is best that you continue with this non-smoking request. It will be reinforcing for you as well as setting a good example for others.

From now on, always sit in the nonsmoking sections of restaurants. This is an affirmation of your *SCOREing* program, and a good habit for avoiding secondary smoke.

When you get up in the morning, stand in front of your bathroom mirror. Look yourself in the eyes, and say the following words out loud *three times*: "Yesterday I stopped using tobacco forever. I am a nonsmoker and I am very happy and excited about that!"

Sometime during the evening, read the following out loud to yourself: "I have now completed my first full day without using tobacco of any kind. This is how it is going to be every day for the rest of my life because I want to feel good, be healthy, and set a good example for others. I am pleased with myself for being a nonsmoker."

Then cross off another successful day on your calendar.

Third Through Thirtieth Day: For each day from Day 3 through Day 30, do the following:

When you go into the bathroom in the morning, look into the mirror and say out loud, "Hi there, nonsmoker. I'm pleased with you for not smoking."

Then sometime during the day, at a time of your choosing, read the following out loud to yourself. You may read it more often than once a day if you wish, but just once is okay. Any time during the day is fine, but just before bedtime is especially good.

"I have succeeded in being a nonsmoker for another day, and I have chosen to be a nonsmoker for many reasons. I know smoking is harmful to my health, and since I only have one life to live I want to live it with the best health I possibly can. I know that smoking gives my breath and my clothing an offensive odor, and I have too much self-respect to want to be a smelly person. I know that smoking can be harmful and unpleasant to other people, and I have no right to inflict harm or unpleasantness on them. Most importantly, I know that if I smoke I am turning control of my life over to a few ounces of dried tobacco leaves that can ruin my health, lessen my vitality, and kill me!

"I need to be controlling my entire life myself. It just doesn't make any sense for an intelligent person like me to allow a few ounces of dried, smoldering leaves to make major decisions concerning my health and self-esteem. Therefore, I have permanently declared myself to be a nonsmoker. I have taken total control of my life and am pleased with myself for this decision. I really like being a nonsmoker, and it feels good to me."

At the end of each day, cross off one more day as a successful nonsmoking day on your calendar. After the 30th day, read the statement out loud to yourself once a week for six more weeks. After that you can stop *SCOREing* if you wish, or you can do it occasionally if you feel the need, because you are a nonsmoker.

—End of *SCOREing* Approach #7B

This may seem like a long *SCOREing* program to you, but it will go quickly. After all, it's likely that you programmed yourself to be a smoker over many months or years. You are now turning that around in a relatively short time. Be assured, your mind is powerful enough to do it. You only need to tell your mind what you want by *SCOREing*.

During the days of your nonsmoking *SCOREing* you may feel the urge to smoke. Combat those urges with *SCOREing* or chewing gum or a toothpick. You could also get involved in an activity to distract your mind from the urge. Getting an urge does not mean the program is not working. The program *is* working, but your mind may rebel for a while like a stubborn child who is told to stop doing something he or she wants to do.

You would not give in and let a child do something that can be harmful, such as playing on the railroad tracks, would you? Of course not. So don't give in to your mind's urges to want to "play on the railroad tracks" (continuing to smoke) either. Don't stand there and let the "train" kill you. Get out of harm's way—*stop smoking by SCOREing.*

"**B**e assured, your mind is power-ful enough to help you accomplish your goal. You only need to tell your mind what you want by SCOREing, and then take appro-priate action."

—Bill Wayne

"Every day in every way, I'm getting better and better! Every day in every way, I'm feeling better and better. Yes, I am. Yes, I am. Yes, I am!"

—Emile Coue

-6-

If Life Hands You a Lemon, Make Lemonade!

SCOREing With Positive Declarations

*"The pessimist sees the difficulty in every opportunity;
the optimist sees the opportunity in every difficulty."*
—L. P. Jacks—

The entire *SCOREing* concept and practice I describe in this book began for me in early 1972. At that time I started giving myself daily instructions, through positive declarations, for my general benefit. What got me started on this was the work of the French psychotherapist Emile Coue (1857-1926). Coue instructed his patients to say to themselves every day, "Every day in every way, I'm getting better and better! Every day in every way, I'm feeling better and better. Yes, I am. Yes, I am. *Yes, I am!*"

And, indeed, Coue's patients did get better and better! So, I thought, "Why not me?" I started saying Coue's positive declarations out loud to myself every day, usually while driving.

Coue's statement is generic and all encompassing, so I didn't know specifically what, if anything, to expect. Within just a few weeks, though, my life began to change profoundly. Unexpected things happened—like losing my job after 18 years of service! In retrospect, being ejected from that job was one of the best things that has ever happened to me. At the time, however, it surely seemed traumatic, but that one event opened up many other possibilities. It kept me moving in the direction of greater fulfillment, prosperity, and happiness.

Concurrently, with all these changes, I began to develop additional positive declarations and included them in my daily *SCOREing*. At first they were generic statements, like Coue's, such as "Positive thoughts benefit me greatly. They help me determine my own destiny as well as expand my abilities in all areas of my life."

Soon, however, I began using positive declarations for *specific* situations. Some of them became quite long, and I had to write them down and read them. (It's really much better to keep them short.) I borrowed the words of others for many of these statements. I used words and concepts from the Bible, Shakespeare, Lincoln, and other renowned sources. I also borrowed heavily from wise sayings and proverbs whose authorships are unknown.

For example, the saying, "If life hands you a lemon, make lemonade," was one I used to develop the following positive declaration when I was out of work: "Life has given me a lemon—I lost my job. I am going to make lemonade out of this situation by finding an exciting, rewarding new career path that is more beneficial to me than anything I have ever done before."

After a few days of repeating the above "lemon-to-lemonade" statement to myself, I had an idea for a new career path. I decided to become a counselor because they use the power of the spoken word to help people overcome challenges. However, I did not know exactly how to transition into counseling. So I just continued repeating the declaration with the belief that the how-to would eventually come along.

A few days later, an idea flashed into my mind: Look up counselor in the phone book and then apply for an apprenticeship. I didn't know if apprenticeships were available or not, but I decided to find out. The phone book listed several counselors. So before making a selection, I repeated the following *SCOREing* statement for several days: "Next Thursday I am going to select a counselor from the phone book for me to interview with, and that person will be the best possible choice for me."

On Thursday I opened the phone book and began reading each counselor's listing out loud, speaking slowly. On one particular name, I felt a quiet feeling of "this is the one." It was a woman whom I shall call Amy Smith.

For several more days prior to visiting Amy, I told myself the following: "When I visit Amy Smith next Monday, I will be confident and relaxed. I will do and say exactly the right things, to demonstrate my knowledge and skill to her, so much so that she will hire me as a trainee."

That Monday was a major turning point in my life. Amy interviewed me in great depth. In her words, "You don't have a degree in psychology or in anything related, but your technical and practical knowledge and your people skills are outstanding. You exceed what I would expect to find in someone with a recent doctorate in psychology. You are hired." (Note that I read extensively and I have a superb memory with a high level of retention.)

Amy trained me as a counselor, and got me started on that exciting, rewarding, and beneficial career path that I had programmed myself for with my *SCOREing*. I soon became even more acutely aware of the power of the spoken word. That led me to continue to expand the scope of the *SCOREing* concept, and this book is a result of that work. I have gone far beyond positive declarations as you can see, but such declarations are where it all started.

Early in my career, I created the following lengthy positive declaration (*SCOREing* Approach #8) for myself. Initially I read it out loud to myself once a day for a month. Then I continued reading it out loud to myself once a week for several years! Now I read it out loud as a reinforcement declaration only a couple of times a year. This has been an extremely powerful *SCOREing* session for me, which I will elaborate on shortly. Feel free to use it yourself or modify it to suit your specific situation as you may choose. Or perhaps just use it as a model from which you can construct your own compelling *SCORE-ing* session.

SCOREing Approach #8—*Serving and Succeeding*

"The words I am reading and speaking are a declaration of who I am, my goals and desires, and what I am now doing and will continue to do in my life. This is truth. This is reality, and this is so. The full power, scope, and meaning of these words and the thoughts behind them are recorded permanently and indestructibly in my entire being and at every level of my thinking. These words and their accompanying thoughts create the reality of me in this person identified as Bill Wayne. Every time I say these words, hear these words, read these words, or think these words, the reality of Bill Wayne expressed by the words becomes infinitely more powerful, more immediate, and more effective in every facet of my life.

"I am one of God's children. I do His work with honor, success, distinction, and integrity in whatever ways He gives me the awareness to serve." This prayer by St. Francis of Assisi expresses my feelings in this regard:

Prayer of St. Francis of Assisi

Lord, make me an instrument of Thy Peace.
Where there is hatred, let me sow love.
Where there is injury, pardon.
Where there is doubt, faith.
Where there is despair, hope.
Where there is darkness, light.
Where there is sadness, joy.
Oh Divine Master, grant that I may not so
much seek to be consoled as to console;
to be understood as to understand;
to be loved, as to love;
for it is in giving that we receive,
it is in pardoning that we are pardoned,
and it is in dying that we are born to
Eternal Life. Amen.

"My ability to picture my dream is excellent—clear, powerful, and effective.

"I am in perfect health and balance in all areas of my life—physically, mentally, spiritually, emotionally, socially, financially, as well as in my career or business, and with my family.

"My destiny is to serve humanity with honor, success, and distinction—as a trainer, speaker, and writer, using all my talents, skills, and abilities for the good of mankind. I am already doing this, and each day I do more and more with ever increasing success in every respect—benefiting others as well as myself. I am growing in awareness in all areas of my life, which benefits everyone I reach.

"My thoughts and actions are guided by truth, wisdom, integrity, and love.

"All the money and material wealth and blessings I ever want or need are always mine—even more than I need is always mine so that I may share with others. I am thankful for the wealth, blessings, and enrichment in all aspects of my life, which are available to all who set goals, believe they can achieve them, and work diligently toward them.

"I am financially independent, physically sound, capable, mentally alert, intelligent, and wise. I am also emotionally stable and mature, and I am following my dream.

"I am a winner and a success in the game of life."

— End of *SCOREing* Approach #8

Here's an example showing the power of this approach. When I created it, I had not yet written this book. I didn't even know what I would, or could, write about. Now I am a published author. I have also been successful as a lecturer and I'm now financially independent. And my dream is to continue writing and speaking to help others achieve their dreams.

Are words powerful? Is *SCOREing* powerful? I think you know the answer. Use your own spoken words to become all you can be, and accomplish what you desire.

The balance of this chapter contains some material that might be beneficial to you in developing your own positive declarations for *SCOREing*. Some of you may want to use this material as is. Others may want to use a concept from which to develop the declarations just as I did with the "lemon-to-lemonade" saying. Start the habit of writing down or memorizing quotations and ideas from good, positive sources. At various times they can be valuable in your *SCOREing*.

The following are just a small sampling of all the material I have drawn on at one time or another, and still do today. I find these inspirational quotes help me keep my thinking straight, and my perspective in balance. They also enable me to be inspired to continually progress in every area of my life:

On Persistence
- "Press on. Nothing in the world can take the place of persistence. Talent will not; nothing is more common than unsuccessful people with talent. Genius will not; unrewarded genius is almost a proverb. Education alone will not; the world is full of educated derelicts. Persistence and determination alone are omnipotent."

—Calvin Coolidge

On Risk Taking
- "There are many ways to fail, but never taking a chance is the surest way. I will, therefore, take a chance on myself, and I will not fail. Instead I will succeed in everything I set my mind and energies on. I will never give up, but will always press on with courage and faith in myself."

—Bill Wayne

On Personal Achievement
- "I shall pass through this world but once. Any good therefore that I can do or any kindness that I can show to any human being, let me do it now. Let me not defer or neglect it, for I shall not pass this way again."

—Author Unknown

On Self-Control
- "I have full control over all my faculties at all times."

—Bill Wayne

On Choice

- "God asks no man whether he will accept life. That is not the choice. You must take it. The only choice is how."

  —Henry Ward Beecher

- "I have but one life to live, and I shall live it with honor, success, distinction, and integrity."

  —Bill Wayne

- "Thirteen virtues are necessary for true success: temperance, silence, order, resolution, frugality, industry, sincerity, justice, moderation, cleanliness, tranquility, chastity, and humility."

  —Benjamin Franklin

On Overcoming the "Blues"

- "Life may be tough, but it sure beats the alternative."

  —Bill Wayne

- "The sun always comes out after a storm."

  —Author Unknown

On Maintaining Perspective About Life

- "I am not worried about tomorrow. Tomorrow has not come. Tomorrow may never come. There is only today, and today is mine."

  —Edward FitzGerald

- "To every thing there is a season, and a time to every purpose under heaven.

  A time to be born, and a time to die; a time to plant, and a time to pluck up that which has been planted;

  A time to kill, and a time to heal; a time to break down, and a time to build up;

  A time to weep, and a time to laugh; a time to mourn, and a time to dance;

  A time to cast away stones, and a time to gather stones together; a time to embrace, and a time to refrain from embracing;

  A time to get, and a time to lose; a time to keep and a time to cast away;

A time to rend, and a time to sew; a time to keep silence, and a time to speak;

A time to love, and a time to hate; a time of war, and a time of peace."*

—Ecclesiastes

*At the end of this, I always add, "And by God's grace and love I know there is a time for me." But, of course, you may end it however you see fit.

On Dealing With Challenges

- "No matter what happens, I can handle it in a sensible, mature, and mutually beneficial manner."

—Bill Wayne

On Death and Dying

- "Cowards die many times before their death;
The valiant never taste of death but once.
Of all the wonders I yet have heard,
It seems to me most strange that men should fear;
Seeing that death, a necessary end,
Will come when it will come."

—Shakespeare

"Positive thoughts benefit me greatly. They help me determine my own destiny, and help expand my abilities in all areas of my life."

—Bill Wayne

"**L**earning to speak in public was so beneficial to me that my entire career skyrocketed after completing the class! Overcoming my greatest fear led to my greatest victory."

—Bill Wayne

-7-

Speak Out
With Confidence
SCOREing on Most People's #1 Fear

"Millions of people take the fear of public speaking to their graves. They sacrifice happiness, maximum success in their careers or businesses, and ultimately their potential."
—Steve Ozer—

A decade or so ago, the results of a nationwide survey were published listing the ten top fears of adults in the United States. Among them were things like the fear of death and going to the dentist, neither of which seemed surprising. But the number one fear was a surprise. No one would likely have predicted it. It was the fear of standing up in front of a group of people and talking to them—stage fright, if you will. As the survey found, most adults, at least in the U.S., are petrified at the thought of addressing a group of people!

Since that survey was published, the fear of talking in front of people has occasionally slipped from the number one position. It was replaced by being in a car crash, having cancer, and a few others, but it has always been in the top ten, year after year. Then in a 1999 survey, talking in front of people returned to the number one position and continues to remain a major fear. This is a shame. Public speaking is one of the most satisfying and rewarding experiences anyone can ever have, yet very few people want to do it—*simply because they are afraid!*

In 1962, I was earning a modest living as a technical writer trainee with IBM. It was readily apparent to me that I would probably retire in that same position unless I learned how to make myself more valuable to the company. It was also clear from my observations that those who were moving up in the company were confident, outgoing people who could speak easily and authoritatively in front of a group. I decided to turn myself into one of those people, so I signed up for the Dale Carnegie Course in Public Speaking and Human Relations.

The course was one night a week for four hours, over a 14-week stretch. One of the requirements was that each student had to speak in front of the class for two minutes at least twice each night.

On the first night, we had to stand in front of the class and tell our name, occupation, and some personal facts, such as hobbies, until the two minutes passed. One student was so petrified that he physically could not move his lips. In two minutes, all he managed to do was mumble his name through trembling lips. The instructor asked him where he worked, but the hapless student could not remember. Later, he told us that those were the longest, most challenging two minutes he had ever spent in his life. Fourteen weeks later, however, he was an articulate speaker who loved public speaking.

Learning to speak in public was so beneficial to me that my entire career skyrocketed after completing the class! *Overcoming my greatest fear led to my greatest victory, and you can have the same results as well!*

Within four years, I had advanced through three significant promotions: from associate writer to senior associate writer to department manager. Within two years after that, I moved up two more levels: from project manager to development manager. And that was just the beginning. Today, I'm an author and speaker. All this took place because I had learned how to speak in front of groups back in 1962, and have enjoyed doing so ever since. It has made all the difference in my life.

You, too, can have a similar success story to tell when you invest a few minutes a day performing *SCOREing* Approaches #9A and #9B, as explained in this chapter. They can help you overcome any stage fright you may have, while gaining immense self-confidence as a result.

These two approaches were developed because most people have not attended a professional public-speaking class as I did. I make no pretense that they are a 100 percent substitute for the kind of intensive in-class training I received. My training went beyond public speaking to include human relations. For most people, however, these approaches will be sufficient for them to get out of any shell they may be in. They can enable almost anyone to have the courage to stand up and say what they think in front of a group of people, and then feel great about themselves for having done so.

The two approaches you are about to read will help prepare you mentally and emotionally for the experience of talking in front of a group of people. They do not teach you how to talk—only actual experience can do that. But *SCOREing* helps you get rid of any fear or apprehension you may have, enabling you to sincerely look forward to talking in front of a group. Actually putting it into practice personally and professionally is up to you.

Now, let's consider some of the many opportunities you may have to speak to groups that you could encounter in your everyday life:

1. At work in department meetings, you could be asked to give a presentation concerning some aspect of your job. More commonly, you are a member of the group and you want to participate by asking questions or offering comments. This is a great way to start out.
2. At PTO (Parent/Teacher Organization) meetings, either as a leader or as an active group participant.
3. In politics, there are many opportunities to talk in front of groups and you need to be good at it to have the chance of advancing in that arena. Politicians will talk anytime anywhere, at the drop of a hat. Unfortunately, many people are elected

because of their public speaking ability even though they may have little else to offer. If you feel you can truly make a difference in politics, you also need to have compassion for others, honesty, integrity, knowledge, and common sense.

4. As a Boy Scout or Girl Scout leader.
5. As a Sunday school class teacher.
6. As an adult education class teacher.
7. As a member of an amateur theater group.
8. In building your career or business, you may need to give presentations in front of prospective clients, customers, and associates. The most successful people are those who can speak in front of others and inspire them to take action.

Now, of course, this list could be made quite a bit longer. Nearly everyone, at sometime in life, has the opportunity to "give his or her two cents worth" to a group of people. However, most people never exercise this opportunity to share. Instead, they allow their fear of speaking to take over, preventing them from saying what they'd like to say. In their minds and hearts they have some important things to say and accomplish as a result, but it seems as though they have trouble getting a grip on their courage, and thus can't seem to get their mouths to work.

Have you ever noticed that those who do open their mouths and speak are often the ones who make things happen? In many cases, they gain the admiration of others, feel good about themselves for speaking up, and they're more likely to get what they want! The ones who have "lockjaw" do not make their ideas known to the group and usually don't get what they want. They rarely make anything happen and, ironically, are often the ones who complain about what is happening *to* them. There is a direct correlation between speaking and success. So start *SCOREing* and speaking, and be a bigger success! Here's how to begin:

1. Perform *SCOREing* Approach #9A—Modify it to suit and do it until you're committed. It's a two-minute talk in which you tell who you are, what you want to accomplish, and why you want to speak to groups of people.

2. Perform *SCOREing* Approach #9B—This consists of some short statements you need to say daily for one month. Thereafter, say them at least once a week until you become comfortable and confident with the idea of speaking to groups of people. Your fear will gradually fade away and you'll actually learn to love to speak.

SCOREing Approach #9A is a sample script for a two-minute talk as a pattern for you to follow. You will, of course, need to create your own script for your own situation. The purpose of Approach #9A is to clearly commit yourself to moving on and speaking in public. Without the commitment, there would be little value in repeating the positive declarations in Approach #9B.

When you give your two-minute *SCOREing* speech, stand up to reinforce your self-confidence. Standing tall gives you a powerful, confident presence in front of others.

You have several great options. Choose whichever one would work best for you:

1. Stand in front of a mirror, and give the presentation to yourself.
2. Stand up and talk into an audio recorder, which you can then play back to hear yourself.
3. Give your presentation to your pet. (But don't be discouraged if it yawns or sleeps through it!)
4. Have friends or family members be your audience, and give your presentation to them.
5. Have a friend or family member capture you on video tape. Do not be concerned if you think you look terrible when you review the video. Be encouraged; most people think they look awful at first. Many professional actors and actresses refuse to view any of the movies they have appeared in for the same reason—they think they look or sound terrible. These are human reactions and are quite normal.

SCOREing Approach #9A—*Moving on and Speaking*
"My name is Mark Anderson, and I've been an electrical engineer for 15 years. The job is getting to be a grind, and I'm not really living how I'd like to.

"I want more control over my life, so I can spend more time with my family and do some traveling. To accomplish that, I have started my own business.

"The friend who shared the business opportunity with me assured me I didn't need any previous business experience. He said all I needed was a dream. Since I had that, I jumped on it, while still working my job.

"Even though I'm just starting out, I know I want to be successful at it and advance to leadership. I'd even like to give seminars to teach and inspire others.

"To achieve my goals, I need to be able to present myself well verbally to people, both men and women, from all walks of life—some of whom I know, and many of whom I don't. This is why I want to overcome all of my apprehensions about public speaking and learn to present myself verbally with confidence and ease.

"We have a regional seminar next month in which a top leader will discuss how we can improve our relationships and accelerate the growth of our business. I am eager to learn, I'll take copious notes for study and application, and I'll also tape it if it's appropriate to do so.

"I intend to use *SCOREing* diligently to prepare myself for this important seminar, and do whatever it takes to succeed. Then I can grow to become one of the leaders who speaks at those seminars. I'm fired up."

— End of *SCOREing* Approach #9A

Now go ahead and prepare your own presentation for your own situation. You may write it out if you wish. You may read it, or memorize it and recite it from memory, or speak extemporaneously— whatever is most comfortable for you. The most important thing, though, is to *do it*. Commit yourself to a specific path of self-development.

There are some sample positive declarations in *SCOREing* Approach #9B to reinforce your presentation in Approach #9A, and to condition your mind for public speaking. It is your choice where you say them—while stopped at a traffic light or in a slow line of traffic; in the bathtub or shower; while working in the yard; while in front of a mirror, family or friends; or in front of your pet. Just do it daily. It only takes a minute or so.

SCOREing Approach #9B—*Speaking in Public*

"My thoughts and opinions are just as valuable as anyone else's. In fact, sometimes my ideas are better than other people's."

"I have a strong desire to express my ideas to groups of people, and I shall do so at every opportunity."

"I am confident in my ability to express my ideas at any time and in any place."

"I have something worthwhile to say, and I say it with confidence."

"I am calm and relaxed every time I speak in public."

"I enjoy expressing myself in public because it helps me become a more fulfilled and successful person."

The preceding statements are a few examples to get you started. Build on these examples to create your own tailored statements that suit your own needs.

—End of *SCOREing* Approach #9B

The secret to success in *SCOREing*, like anything else, is practice, persistence, and determination.

SCOREing to overcome stage fright is especially powerful to use with family, friends, coworkers, and business associates. Since many people have the fear of public speaking, it is likely you know someone who also has this fear. Get a group together and each of you do *SCOREing* in the presence of the others. Have fun with it. You will all benefit greatly. You could even expand to create more *SCOREing* presentations about various topics. For example, pick a topic such as success, happiness, marriage, business, and so forth. Then each of you can share your ideas in a two-minute *SCOREing* exercise.

One rule: No criticism! The only purpose is to give you each a forum to practice expressing yourself in front of others.

You can, of course, use *SCOREing* on various subjects by yourself. You don't need to have others present. Keep in mind that you are training yourself to express your ideas out loud, so that you will be able to do so more effectively each time you have an opportunity.

If the PTO chairperson asks, "Tom or Mary, what do you think about the school lunch program?" you will be so conditioned that you will stand up, smile, and say, "I think...." Then you'll go on to say what you think. You will speak with confidence because you have trained yourself well and improved your skill at speaking up through *SCOREing.*

As you proceed in your efforts to overcome any stage fright you may have, you'll become an excellent, self-assured public speaker. Best wishes and great *SCOREing. You can do it!*

"Have you ever noticed that those who open their mouths and speak are often the ones who make things happen? There is a direct correlation between speaking and success. So start SCORE-ing and speaking, and be a bigger success!"

—Bill Wayne

"**S**COREing can help you better prepare yourself for giving a presentation, thus increasing your chances for having someone become a new friend, buy from you, or associate with you."

—Bill Wayne

-8-

A Presentation Is a Two-Way Street
SCOREing for an Excellent Presentation

"The men whom I have seen succeed
have always been cheerful and hopeful, who went about
their business with a smile on their faces, and took the changes and
chances of this mortal life like men."
—Charles Kingsley—

Presentation is about what you do and how you do it every day when you interact with other people. At the most basic level, when you have a face-to-face conversation with someone, you present yourself by your tone of voice, use of words, body language, and facial expressions. To have effective communication—perhaps to convince the other person of your point of view—you need to do all of this with excellence.

In the business world, presentations take on a larger dimension of communication. There are presentations where you may speak to a group of fellow workers, associates, executives, clients, or customers. You may use a whiteboard, flipcharts, slides, Power Point, or other exhibits to enhance your presentation. But regardless of how sophisticated the presentation becomes, the goal is the same—to have effective communication, otherwise known as a two-way exchange of information. Businesspeople present their product, service, or opportunity, and hope to get feedback from the prospect, client, customer, or associate. Teachers present information to the class and anticipate feedback from their students, usually in the form of asking and answering questions.

All successful presenters know their success depends largely on how well they present themselves personally. Anyone who dresses sloppily or talks crudely is not likely to be very successful regardless of how good his or her product, service, or opportunity is, or how fascinating the subject of discussion may be. As our economy shifts to people opting for more control over their lives by running their own home-based businesses, presenting is becoming more important. So *SCOREing Approach #10* will deal with presenting an opportunity. But this approach can be used as a model for any type of presentation.

If you are typical and have been fortunate enough to have been given an opportunity yourself, presenting that opportunity to others is probably not an experience you have looked forward to, at least initially. *SCOREing* can help you better prepare for giving a presentation, thus increasing your chances for having someone become a friend, buy from you, or associate with you. But before I get into *SCOREing* a presentation, let me digress for a moment to briefly cover some other aspects of presenting. If you fail to do your best on these, all the *SCOREing* in the world may not save the day for you.

You have probably heard the expression, *"You'll never get a second chance to make a good first impression."* Yes, your first impression is most important. It's the one that will permeate the entire presentation. Make a great first impression, and it can cancel out some minor goofups you might make during the presentation. Make a negative first impression, and it can cancel out many of the excellent things you might say during the presentation.

Five Rules for Making a Terrific First Impression
1. Be on time for the presentation. Being 15-20 minutes ahead of time is even better because it gives you time to shift gears, do

any last minute preparation, perhaps rehearse a little, and focus on what you're about to do.

2. Be neat and clean, but don't dress like a fashion model. Just wear clean, pressed clothing. Look like you own a business. Use good taste, and lean toward the conservative side, color and style-wise. You'll be less likely to offend others.

3. Take care of your personal hygiene. No body odor or dragon-mouth please. There is no excuse in our society for not complying with this.

4. Do not smoke.

5. For men, it's best to be clean-shaven. One-third of the population mistrusts men with facial hair.

In my many years in management, I interviewed countless numbers of people. I had some job seekers who flagrantly violated the first three rules. Three cases that come to mind are:

1. An electrical engineer showed up an hour and a half late for a 10:30 a.m. appointment because he "overslept." He did not bother to phone either.

2. A woman showed up in a see-through blouse. She was not even wearing a bra.

3. A man showed up reeking of body odor so strong I could smell him before I could see him. When he got close enough to speak, his breath was even more foul than his body odor.

As you can imagine, none of these three people were hired! I personally have not had anyone violate rule number 4, probably because I had a prominent "No Smoking" sign in my office. And I don't recall ever hiring anyone with facial hair! Forewarned is forearmed. Follow the above five rules and make a great first impression. Let's assume you will abide by the preceding rules. What else do you need to do, for example, if you're in sales or building a business?

1. Be so helpful and friendly that the prospect will know that you're the person he or she wants to buy from or associate with.

2. Share enough information about the company, its product, service, and opportunity, and the potential for the prospect to solve his or her problem, or otherwise benefit by buying from or associating with you.
3. Identify that person's dream, goal, or objective. Find out what the prospect really wants and let him or her know that your product, service, or opportunity could be what he or she needs to accomplish it.

Many presenters ignore the third item because they think others just want or need to know how to do something. But if you ignore the prospect's dream, goal, or objective, you'll have an excellent chance of not being successful with him or her. You'll probably be disappointed by the prospect's response and end up losing his or her interest. Maximize having the person buy from or associate with you by finding out what his or her dream, goal, or objective is—*and focusing on it.* Everyone first needs a reason why before that individual will move forward on anything. As time goes on, the how-to aspects will virtually take care of themselves—and the prospect will start believing you can help him or her solve a problem or otherwise realize a dream, goal, or objective.

SCOREing can be quite useful in helping you prepare to give a successful presentation. It can help you sell yourself as you share your product, service, or opportunity. One caution: *SCOREing* will help you only if *you* have enough desire to overcome a challenge, or achieve a dream, goal, or objective. And the prospect must have the desire to take advantage of what you're offering. Otherwise *SCOREing,* or anything else you might do, is likely to get you nowhere fast with that person. However, always be alert to the possibility that he or she may be able to lead you to others who *do* have sufficient desire to take action. To *SCORE successfully,* you need to be committed to *your* dreams, goals, and objectives *first,* and go through the numbers to find others who see and seize what you have to share.

Even when you are committed, though, you may still need to overcome certain tendencies that might have worked against you. For example, excessive nervousness, lack of self-confidence, talking too much, not talking enough, displaying a negative or defeatist attitude, not listening, or not showing sincere interest or enthusiasm for what you are doing could lead to a no. But you can develop *SCOREing* sessions to deal with these matters.

You can overcome with these potential challenges by having a few simple *SCOREing* sessions prior to giving the presentation. *SCOREing* Approach #10 is a generic *SCOREing* session that you can tailor to suit your specific situation. If you have several days before the presentation, read it out loud at least twice a day, every day. If you have only one day, or only a few hours, read Approach #9B (see page 79) at least three times aloud.

One strong recommendation: Find out as much about the prospect as you can in advance and write down specific important questions to ask him or her.

SCOREing Approach #10—*Sharing an Opportunity*

"On (state the date and time) I am sharing my business opportunity with a qualified prospect.

"During the presentation I will be relaxed and calm, yet enthusiastic. I am confident I can share my opportunity with excellence, and I shall display my confidence by leading the prospect.

"I will talk easily and comfortably and answer all questions as honestly and fully as I can.

"I will show that I care by listening attentively, asking questions about the prospect, and helping that person build his or her dream or state and elaborate on his or her goal or objective. I will balance my talking and listening appropriately.

"Here are the benefits of my opportunity and what I have to offer the prospect, if he or she qualifies." (Here you will state what qualities the prospect has and what advantages your opportunity has to offer him or her. You need to state these qualifications to yourself in detail: enthusiasm, desire, personal strengths, and such.)

"Here are some questions I definitely want to ask the prospect:" (Here state the specific questions you want the prospect to answer for you. You need to have them already written down.)

"I am now confident, prepared, and ready, for my presentation with (name of the person) on (day and time). I know I will present myself in the best manner possible and will make a strong, positive I-care-about-you impression on my prospect."

— End of *SCOREing* Approach #10

SCOREing Approach #10 is quite simple and to the point. In essence, it is a mock presentation. Pretend you are presenting to someone when you do this approach. Put some enthusiasm and drama into your words when you share your opportunity and do what you need to do to have your best chance of getting a yes. Have fun with it! Encourage the invisible prospect to associate with you because you have a vehicle that can help that person make his or her dream come true or reach a goal or objective. The more enthusiasm you can work up as you *SCORE* the better. Speaking the words with emotion will make an even deeper impression on your mind.

The more times you run through a *SCOREing* session like this, the greater your chances are for making a good, solid impression on the prospect when you give the actual presentation. *SCOREing* prepares you to do your best. It impregnates your mind with the thoughts and facts that you want to remember during the presentation. Then when you get into the actual presentation you do not have the stress of endeavoring to think fast about what to do or say because it is already in your mind. Your presentation will be more like a casual, yet important, conversation between two friends.

One reason actors and actresses seem so natural in their roles is because they have practiced them *out loud,* many times prior to their actual performances. A presentation is a performance, and you are the actor or actress playing yourself. Use *SCOREing* to get the practice you need to warm up and become comfortable with your role—then you can more easily give an award-winning performance. The potential reward will be having your prospect say "Yes! I'm excited."

"A presentation is a performance, and you are the actor or actress playing yourself. Use SCOREing to get the practice you need to warm up and become comfortable with your role—then you can more easily give an award-winning performance. The potential reward will be having your prospect say, 'Yes! I'm excited.'"

—Bill Wayne

"**G**raciously give and receive love and openly appreciate others. Set an example which creates ripples of positive change. When enough people do this, it will become the accepted thing to do, and the followers will have better role models to emulate."

—Bill Wayne

-9-

You Can't Push a Rope but You Can Gently Pull a Wet Noodle!

SCOREing Destructive Prejudice Out of Your Life

*"I could tell where the lamplighter was
by the trail he left behind him."*
—Harry Lauder–

Two of the dictionary's primary definitions for prejudice are: 1) An unfavorable opinion or feeling formed beforehand or without knowledge, thought, or reason. 2) Any preconceived opinion or feeling either favorable or unfavorable.

The first definition above is an insidious malignancy that needs to be eliminated from all societies and nations in the world today. We need to stop the prejudice which has caused, and continues to cause death, social imprisonment, and subjugation of millions of innocent, decent human beings. Instead, we need to embrace our differences and be glad we aren't all alike. That would be pretty boring, don't you agree?

No one is exempt from prejudice. It seems that most of us are in a minority group of some sort, which apparently qualifies us to be a candidate for prejudice. Here are some of the prominent minority groups: religion, race, nationality, age, hair color, physical and mental challenges, geographical location, skin color, educational level, political beliefs, appearance, family name, occupation, socioeconomic position, and gender. Within these groups there are often subgroups of minorities. For example, within religion there are many diverse groups, each of which may harbor prejudice against others in other groups.

Prejudice is destructive, senseless, and needless—it just doesn't do anyone any good. Fortunately, there is something each of us, individually, can do about it. We can make our best effort to keep ourselves in balance and free of prejudice. We can use *SCOREing* to tune ourselves up so we can welcome and appreciate the differences in ourselves and others.

Graciously give and receive love and openly appreciate others. Set an example which creates ripples of positive change. When enough people do this, it will become the accepted thing to do, and the followers will have better role models to emulate. In a few moments you will learn about *SCOREing* Approach #11, which will help you to be one of the leaders of the pack of this positive change and make a difference.

First, though, let's examine the second definition of prejudice: "Any preconceived opinion or feeling, either favorable or unfavorable." Within the scope of this definition there is room for a positive, constructive kind of prejudice. There is a strong need in our society for a powerful prejudice against greed, crime, drunken driving, and violence. We need to be prejudiced against anything that unjustly deprives another human being or creature of his or her rights. With *SCOREing* we can create this positive kind of prejudice within ourselves. In so doing, we strengthen our own character and contribute to a stronger, more peaceful society.

Most of us really don't believe we are prejudiced against other groups of people. I don't think I am. However, if we take a closer look, we'll often find we are mistaken about this. It is a challenge to be absolutely certain, under all circumstances, that we didn't pick up or create some prejudice along the way.

So let's not take chances, and let's keep ourselves tuned up and tuned in "just in case." It only takes a few minutes, and it can help make us and society stronger and better for it. I believe I am an accepting person and, still, I frequently give myself these tune-ups.

Let's eliminate destructive prejudices and replace them with acceptance and appreciation, by using *SCOREing* Approach #11. As with all *SCOREing* approaches, you may want to alter it to suit your specific situation. Do this approach as often as you wish but at least once a month. If having destructive prejudice is a situation in your life, do the approach daily until you get tuned up.

Read the following out loud to yourself. And, if you are so inclined, you may want to include your family and other group participants as well.

SCOREing Approach #11—Eliminating Harmful Prejudices

"I respect the rights and beliefs of all people without exception, as long as their actions do not deprive others of *their* rights.

"I vow to always be supportive, in my thoughts, words, and actions, of the rights of all individuals and groups of people.

"I strive to learn more about people and groups who are different from me. This will help me better understand, respect, and harmonize with them.

"Whenever I encounter prejudice, I do whatever I can to counteract it.

"By keeping myself tuned up against destructive personal prejudice, I am making a positive difference in the world.

"Here are some good prejudices that I am making a part of my character: I am prejudiced against greed, crime, drunken driving, social injustice, and violence. I am prejudiced against any word or action that deprives another human being of his or her rights.

"I extend my thoughts and actions to embrace all creatures."

—End of *SCOREing* Approach #11

Up to this point, we have been concerned only with putting ourselves in balance by *SCOREing* out destructive prejudices and

SCOREing in constructive prejudices. But what about the prejudices of other people? What can be done about that?

People always do what they *really* want and are sufficiently motivated to do; you have no control over that. Trying to force another person to change is like trying to *push* a rope uphill—it simply cannot be done. However, it is possible to gently *pull* a wet noodle!

So what's the point? Trying to force someone into doing something is like trying to push a rope uphill. It's a losing proposition. Getting someone to change can be even harder than pushing a rope uphill, especially if he or she is being particularly stubborn. But did you ever try to pull a wet noodle? If you pull too quickly or too hard, the noodle will break and not pull free in one piece. Getting another person to change is like trying to pull just one wet noodle from a pile of wet noodles without breaking the noodle you're pulling on. You need to pull on it very gently, so it doesn't break!

When you have an optimistic attitude, show a positive example, and maintain a supportive environment, others are more likely to want to follow you. They will be the wet noodles you can gently pull. As the saying goes, "You can't push a rope, but you can gently pull a wet noodle." So free yourself of prejudice by using *SCOREing* Approach #11 above. Become a shining example—by your compassionate, accepting words and actions—for others to follow.

When you encounter prejudice, stand against it in an empathetic, non-confrontative way, if at all possible. Have your presentation take the form of a sincere conversation. Use it to discover why the person harbors the prejudice he or she has and gently offer a counter viewpoint for his or her consideration, without being argumentative. Plant non-prejudice seeds in the mind of the person who is being prejudicial. *When* you set a great example by freeing yourself of prejudice, and *when* you *SCORE* a non-confrontational presentation, you have an excellent chance of pulling the wet noodle.

Will you, all by yourself, be able to eliminate all hate and prejudice in the world? No! No one person can do this. However, you do have the power to eliminate any prejudice *you* may have. Be someone to emulate—especially for those who are sorely in need of a positive role model. Such an uplifting influence will expand to affect more and more people. When your loving, accepting thinking and behavior catches on, even if it's just with one person at a time, the world will be a better place.

We have not done away with prejudice yet, but this is an excellent start. Just let it begin with *you*! Then gently start pulling some wet noodles today.

"*From time to time, spouses have disagreements. Fortunately, this is normal and can even be beneficial when handled with love. Expressing opposite perspectives can be helpful, enabling spouses to better understand each other and themselves too. SCOREing can help couples work through disagreements in a positive, constructive way. This not only can help resolve issues, but also bring the spouses closer together.*"

—Bill Wayne

-10-

Be Quiet and Listen to Each Other

SCOREing for Peace with Your Spouse

"Love is not blind—it sees more, not less.
But because it sees more, it is willing to see less."
—Julius Gordon—

Certainly one of the most challenging situations for any married person to deal with successfully is an emotionally charged disagreement with his or her spouse.

Have you ever felt like screaming at your spouse, telling him or her to be quiet—that they don't know what they're talking about? Perhaps you have actually screamed some harsh remarks at your spouse. If you have, you know where it has gotten you—nowhere pleasant. Such remarks only escalate emotional intensity to a higher level and lead to less intelligent communication. When negative emotions enter the scene, intelligence and control usually leave.

From time to time, spouses have disagreements. Fortunately, this is normal and can bring the relationship to a higher level when handled with love. Expressing opposite perspectives can be helpful, enabling spouses to better understand each other and themselves too. *SCOREing* can help couples work through disagreements in a positive, constructive way. This not only can help resolve issues, but also bring spouses closer together.

However, if disagreements are not handled in a loving, mature, and rational manner they can become extremely harmful and destructive to both parties. If they evolve into screaming matches, mean accusations, nasty remarks, or even into physical violence, they are always harmful and destructive. The participants degrade their own humanity and do great harm to not only their own self-esteem, respectively, but to each other's as well. Those in a relationship who scream and shout harsh remarks at each other are injuring rather than nourishing their relationship.

The more damage done to the relationship the more handling disagreements is a serious matter. Yet, there are some self-proclaimed experts who promote open confrontation as a solution to disagreements. They profess we should say exactly what we think and feel without regard to the other person's feelings. They promote face-to-face screaming matches as a solution to problems.

I once saw a television program where one of these so-called experts showed videos of mean-spirited, heated confrontations between husbands and wives, which he actually encouraged in his clients. The abusive, degrading language and voice tones used were horrible. And knowing it was for real—not just actors playing their parts—made it quite disturbing to watch.

The actual participants were then interviewed by the so-called expert who asked each one of them the same question: "How did it make you feel to get your anger and frustration off your chest?" The participants said that they felt good about getting everything out in the open.

"There, you see," the expert said, "this is really good therapy." The show's host, however, apparently was not buying it and asked, "Are all of you now happily married?" One hundred percent of them answered that they were divorced shortly after the encounter shown on the video. One woman said that even though she felt good about getting things off her chest, she was so deeply hurt by her husband's remarks that it caused the divorce. "I could never forget those terrible things he said to me."

"I didn't mean it the way it sounded," he defended. "I was just letting off steam like you were."

Then the other participants chimed in to say that they had felt exactly the same way—they had enjoyed letting off steam, but, on the other hand, at the end of the segment, had felt deeply hurt by their respective spouses remarks.

The host gave the "expert" a glance that said, "Who are you trying to fool? This stuff is harmful, not helpful."

The expert's claim to fame was that he had a doctorate degree and, by inference, was infallible. But I disagree 100 percent with this so-called expert's approach to solving personal disagreements. Having a Ph.D. degree does not, in and of itself, qualify a person for anything. In matters of personal counseling, common sense and a caring heart are much more important—two things the "expert" lacked.

The truth is quite evident. Words are extremely powerful, and once they are spoken they cannot be retrieved or canceled. So, whenever you speak to someone or to yourself, choose your words wisely. For example, there is a world of difference between saying, "You are stupid!" and "You behaved in a not-so-good manner at the party last night!" In the first statement, you are assaulting a person's self-esteem by saying he or she has a serious defect and is an unacceptable human being. In the second statement, you are reminding someone that he or she temporarily behaved in an undesirable manner. There is no assault on his or her worth as a human being. You are simply addressing that person's *behavior*. And remember, a person is *not* their behavior. Consistent behavior though, reflects certain attitudes and habit patterns. The first statement can drive a permanent wedge between you and the other person. The second statement does not.

What this, of course, is all leading up to is *SCOREing* Approach #12. It's a method that promotes healing after a serious disagreement. Credentials needed: common sense and a caring heart. To have a successful healing to a serious, emotionally charged disagreement, you need to achieve four things:

1. You need to get your anger and frustration off your chest in a constructive way.

2. You need to calmly and rationally state your side of the argument as fairly as you can.
3. You need to calmly and rationally state your understanding of the other person's side of the argument as fairly as you can.
4. You need to allow the healing to occur. There are two aspects to this, which will be discussed shortly.

All of the above four things can be successfully achieved through *SCOREing* and usually only one session is needed. Use *SCOREing* Approach #12 as a pattern for you to follow when you devise the scenario for your own situation.

Here's a scenario example to help you get started: You and your spouse are grocery shopping. As you wander through the crowded store together you make small talk about products and prices. You both agree that prices are way out of line and there doesn't seem to be any end in sight. You both wonder how you are going to be able to eat decently within your income if prices continue to increase. Out of curiosity, you pick up a package of T-bone steaks to read the price.

Your spouse sees you, assumes you intend to purchase it, and says in a loud, angry tone that attracts the attention of all the other shoppers in the area, "We can't afford that! If you didn't waste money on books and magazines, we could have a steak! You can't have your books and magazines and a steak too!"

At this point you have several choices:

1. You can yell, "The heck with you!" and stomp out of the store, thus laying the groundwork for a heated argument later.
2. You can yell that your spouse wastes more money than you do, and start itemizing each perceived waste. This would probably escalate the situation into a full-scale war, right then and there, with plenty of spectators.
3. Or, you can think to yourself, "OOPs! This is one I had better handle later with *SCOREing*." Then gently put the steaks back with a soft, calm remark to your spouse, "Just checking the price, not buying." (This gentleness and the empathetic statement will probably start to immediately diffuse any anger.)

You know *something* is bothering your spouse, and it may not even be about the steak. Maybe he or she had a particularly challenging day at work, but this is not the time or place to deal with it. You also know you had better not ignore the situation because it is obviously symptomatic of something. You are consciously buying a little more time until you can be alone first to handle the situation with *SCOREing.*

Here's a *SCOREing* approach for the situation just described. Say out loud to yourself the words in quotations. The other words are for information or explanation. But just remember—*perform this approach only while you are alone and where no one can overhear you.*

SCOREing Approach #12—*Helping to Heal Your Family's Financial Stress*

The first thing you need to do is get rid of any anger you may be feeling. If you need to, yell, scream, or otherwise vent the words. Be emotional. Get it all out. *Just be sure to do this only when you are alone.*

Step One: "What in the world is your problem (spouse's name)? Today in the supermarket you acted as though you didn't have the brains God gave green apples! You embarrassed and humiliated me. Your behavior was totally unacceptable. I do not deserve that sort of verbal abuse and you know it! You accused me of wasting money on books and magazines. Well, I enjoy reading and I have a right to some enjoyment. And what about you? You waste money on...."

Now go through the items (if any) you think are wasteful on your spouse's part... "and I have never denied you anything you enjoy. Let's be fair about this...." Continue to rant and rave out loud to yourself until you have totally exhausted your anger. Point out all the good things you have done. Point out all the things your spouse has done that annoy you. Let it all hang out—*in the safety of your own privacy.*

When your anger and frustration are spent, you will have given yourself a much needed, beneficial emotional catharsis. And no harm has been done to your spouse or the relationship.

Step Two: Now clearly and calmly state your side of the situation—out loud, to yourself:

"I buy one personal development or business book and receive one business magazine a month, which I read, learn from, and enjoy. This costs about (state the cost) a month, which I don't believe hurts us financially. In fact, these publications are helping me grow as a person. I'm also learning more about business and how to become more successful. I believe that by reading them, I can learn how to relate better with others and do things that will improve our financial situation.

"I believe you are angry with me because we are in debt and I'm spending this money. And I truly understand that. But I think we need to look at the cost of these publications as an investment in our future rather than as an expense. I'm glad we're talking about this. Perhaps you and I, together, in a calm and mature manner, need to take some time and go over our entire budget. We might find it to be a good idea to readjust our spending in other areas, so that we use our money as wisely as possible. Why don't we sit down and go over everything together?"

Step Three: Now clearly and calmly state your spouse's side of the situation—out loud to yourself—as fairly as you can:

"You are frustrated with the continuous rise in the cost of living which is outpacing our income. You see my buying books and magazines as a contributing factor to our financial stress. You haven't been enjoying my books or magazines, like I have, which is probably adding to your frustration. You certainly have the right to question the wisdom of how we spend our money in all areas, including money spent on books and magazines."

Step Four: Now you allow the healing to begin. This involves two actions on your part: You first need to analyze the situation based on steps two and three above. Then state your solution—out loud to yourself—and take appropriate action based on it.

Here are two sample *SCOREing* sessions dealing with different situations:

1. "I really am guilty of spending money on books and magazines, which are costing us over $500 a year. I rarely have time to read more than one magazine, sometimes skimming the oth-

ers and sometimes not. I have stacks of back issues that I intend to read someday, which currently take up all the floor space in two closets. I will cancel all magazine subscriptions except one, and discard or give away all the back issues because I know I will never get around to reading all of them. I will focus on reading just one book and one business magazine a month."

2. "I don't believe I read too many books or magazines. I read one book and one magazine a month with a total cost of only $300 a year or so, which I feel is reasonable. I really enjoy reading these publications and I would like to continue doing so. I hope you appreciate my desire in this as I believe they will help us move ahead in life."

Then you go and talk it over with your spouse, saying essentially either (1) or (2) above, or a modification of either, depending on which best reflects the situation.

By the time you start talking to your spouse, the healing will have already made significant progress. It's already 99 percent complete.

—End of *SCOREing* Approach #12

As you can see, the key elements in *SCOREing* Approach #12 are:

1. Be quiet, whether you'd like to start yelling or not. Maintain your self-control.
2. Listen. Really pay attention to the words your spouse is saying, feel his or her emotion, and strive to truly understand what the underlying challenge is.

When you do these two things, the outcome will be a stronger bond between the two of you. You'll be showing your love—that you care—which is a key bonding agent!

Neither of the scenarios above may describe your specific challenge, but they could be helpful models for you to follow in resolving it, whatever it may be. To recap:

1. Purge yourself of anger and frustration. Let it all hang out when you are alone and where no one can hear you. Get it out of your system.
2. State your side of the situation as accurately and fairly as you can, while still alone.
3. State your spouse's side of the situation as accurately and fairly as you can, while you're still alone.
4. Analyze steps 2 and 3, and adopt a solution.
5. Talk out loud to yourself and rehearse what you'll say to your spouse.
6. Finally, talk to your spouse about the solution in a calm, loving tone, and listen closely to what he or she shares. Respond in a kind, caring way, as you work through the situation until it is healed.

Of course, all this needs to be done out loud to yourself in order to gain the benefits of *SCOREing,* as discussed earlier in this book. The power of the *SCOREing* approach is awesome. I have found that after it is used a few times for different situations, serious spousal challenges seem to cease completely, and you may never need to use the program again. It seems to have an all-encompassing influence on you and your spouse to the extent you seem to be able to avoid situations before they become problematic.

"**I** *believe you are angry with me because we are in debt and I am spending this money. And I truly understand that. But I think we need to look at the cost of these publications as an investment in our future rather than as an expense.*"

—Bill Wayne

"Engineers design pressure vessels with safety valves to prevent explosions. But what about us? What do we do to provide a safety valve for ourselves? Most people do nothing, and that is unfortunate, because there are safety valves available that can help."

—Bill Wayne

-11-

Venting Your Frustrations
SCOREing to Release Stress

"When you practice identifying areas of struggle, then root out the struggle response and replace it with positive action, little by little, you will free up your life."
—Danny and Marie Lena—

Most of us live in a multi-faceted, fast-paced world. There are a lot of people and situations to deal with—jobs, bosses, coworkers, spouses, kids, parents, the tax collector, the drive to and from work, the high cost of living, death or illness, and the government. Then there are mechanical malfunctions, long streaks of severe weather, the postal service, the dentist, the doctor, in-laws, relatives, too much exposure to loud or irritating noises, and a million other things. These are all potential sources of stress for someone at any given moment. Whew! This sure demonstrates the need for a positive mental attitude now, doesn't it?

Most of us can handle a certain amount of stress reasonably well most of the time. But some of us have less tolerance for it. We all have had a sufficient amount of stress put on us at some time or other, have felt "maxed out," and needed some help. We may even stop functioning the way we normally do because we are so stressed-out.

If we have too much stress too frequently, it can take a toll on both our mental and physical well-being. We are in danger of be-coming grouchy, negative, depressed, or even mentally ill in extreme cases. Too much stress can even lead to a serious physical reaction, such as a heart attack. Or we may develop some socially unacceptable behavior, such as becoming angry to the point of violence. Stress can be damaging and may even kill you if not dealt with properly.

Be sure to consult your physician concerning stress and how to handle it, as this book is not intended to give medical advice. There is, however, a common sense thing we can all do to help defuse stress before it builds up and becomes a problem. Think of stress as being like pressure in a steam boiler. If the pressure continues to build and there is no safety valve to let some of it out, the boiler will eventually explode, destroying itself and anything nearby. A common pressure cooker has a safety valve that will open and release, or vent, steam at a certain set pressure. Some even have a backup fuse plug that will blow out if the regular safety valve doesn't open when it's supposed to.

Engineers design pressure vessels with safety valves to prevent explosions. But what about us? What can we do to provide a safety valve for ourselves? Most people do nothing, and that is unfortunate, because there are various safety valves available. For instance, perhaps your physician would recommend taking a brisk walk or run, lifting weights, or working out at a gym. And there is another safety valve that can be used, at no cost, and for which you don't need a prescription. It has served me well to relieve my stress and maybe it will do the same for you. It's a special *SCOREing* scenario that you will read about shortly.

First, let's look at the two ways we typically deal with stress:

1. Hold it in. Try to be tough about it. Don't let anyone know how it is tearing us up inside.
2. Release it with no holds barred against anyone or anything that may be close-by.

The first method can build up anger and resentment, eventually harming your health, and even killing you. The second one can cause property damage and mental or physical harm to others. It can also destroy relationships and land you on the wrong side of the law. Stress needs to be periodically released in a non-harmful way. And that's exactly what *SCOREing* Approach #13 can help you do.

SCOREing Scenario for releasing stress: The objective of *SCOREing* Approach #13 is designed so you can help yourself let off steam. This chapter is subtitled "*SCOREing* to Release Stress" because that is exactly what you need to do—vent. Don't just talk out loud to yourself. Turn up the volume. Raise your voice or SHOUT if you need to. Get yourself worked up. Yell or scream whatever comes to mind—in private, of course!

Venting is using your physical and emotional power in a healthy, harmless way. For example, imagine that, today, you experienced a particularly high-pressure situation at work. The drive home was extremely challenging—a two-hour traffic jam in 90-degree weather, and your car's air conditioning system didn't work. Once home, you read a letter from the tax office informing you that you are going to be audited. You have had it! You have had enough of this junk!

SCOREing Approach #13—*Venting Stress and Proclaiming Your Freedom*

Go somewhere private, for example: your garage, in a room with the door closed, in a field or forest, in the mountains, or in a remote part of a city park. The idea is to be by yourself so you can shout out loud to yourself. You are going to yell out your frustrations while you punctuate your words by clenching your fist and hitting the air as if it were a punching bag. You're going to verbally and physically vent. It might go something like this: (BAM indicates you are throwing a punch against the air as hard as you can).

"I'm sick (BAM) and tired (BAM) of being sick and tired! (BAM) I'm tired of always being in debt (BAM). I'm sick and tired of not having enough time to do the things I want to do (BAM). I'm sick and tired of working all the time and not getting ahead (BAM). I'm sick and tired of driving this old car (BAM) and living in this little old house (BAM). In fact, I'm sick and tired of my job (BAM), and I'm ready to move on (BAM)!"

You get the idea? Be creative. Let it all hang out. Be assertive. Let no stone go unturned in your effort to release steam about everything that is annoying you. Anything is fair game. Keep shouting and punching the air, but stop when you feel you have had enough.
—End of *SCOREing* Approach #13

You have released or vented your stress in a beneficial way. You have rejoined the human race and are fit to be around again. You feel better because you are better. Use this *SCOREing* approach to release stress—just to "clean house" and keep "tuned up." It may seem crazy, but it works! If we keep negative feelings inside, they could build up to the point where they cause us to harm a relationship or injure our own health.

"**V**enting is using your physical and emotional power in a healthy, harmless way. If we keep negative feelings inside, they could build up to the point where they cause us to harm a relationship or injure our own health."

—Bill Wayne

"We all like to receive the warm fuzzies, and we all need to look for opportunities to give them to others. Compliments can be powerful when done sincerely. There is nothing more effective than a compliment for encouraging as well as lifting a frayed spirit."

—Bill Wayne

-12-

The Warm Fuzzies
Self-Compliment by *SCOREing*

"To be a top performer, start by believing you already are one. Self-belief whispers, 'Keep doing what you know you need to be doing. Success will come!' Self-belief instills that you have what it takes to win. You know you will reach your goal."
—Tony Sciré—

When someone compliments you on your appearance or behavior, says you have done a good job, or even gives you a big hug "just because," that is commonly called a *warm fuzzy*. We all like to receive the warm fuzzies, and we all need to look for opportunities to give them to others. Compliments can be powerful when done sincerely. There is nothing more effective than a compliment for encouraging as well as lifting a frayed spirit. They're marvelous for building a strong, healthy self-esteem.

I remember the cowboy movies of a few decades ago where heroes and heroines were not allowed to accept compliments. The tall, soft-spoken stranger would ride into town on the way to somewhere else. (In those days, it seems, all the heroes were tall, soft-spoken strangers who just rambled from place to place, seemingly with no job or income.)

Predictably, the town was held in the grips of fear by a host of at least a dozen bad guys. Of course, the tall, soft-spoken stranger took time out to clean up the town all by himself before moving on to the next town. Just before he mounted his horse to leave, the town's good people gathered around and did their best to compliment him. But he was not allowed to accept the kind words. So he just looked down at the ground, kicked a stone with the toe of his boot, and softly said, "Shucks. It weren't nothin," after which he rode out of town into the sunset.

I suppose this was to show that we always need to be humble. And I agree with that. We do need to have humility, just as the truly successful do. However, gracefully accepting a compliment does *not* make us lose our humility. In fact, it honors the person bestowing it upon us. It's bragging that's not humble. It is carrying self-complimenting to an unacceptable, prideful extreme. And no one likes to be around someone who boasts about themselves and their accomplishments. But, I'll just bet that when the tall, soft-spoken stranger rode far enough from town so no one could hear, he halted his horse. He probably said out loud to himself (alone, other than being on his horse), "You did a good job, Slim." Then he rode on to clean up the next town.

It takes a healthy self-esteem to tackle the challenges we face every day and overcome the obstacles that surface along the way to accomplishing our dreams and goals. Self-esteem feeds on compliments for nourishment but, more often than not, few people seem to give them. Therefore, in many cases, you need to compliment yourself if you want to be a winner in life. Yes, self-complimenting is okay! In fact, it is required for good self-esteem. Our tall, soft-spoken stranger knew that in his heart when he said out loud in private, "You did a good job, Slim."

SCOREing Approach #14—*Complimenting Yourself*
Start today and continue every day, for the rest of your life, to give yourself a *warm fuzzy* in private. Say out loud to yourself, "You did a great job, (your name)," "You are a champion, (your name)," "You have what it takes to do anything you set your mind to, (your name)," or some other similar simple, self-complimentary

statement. That is all there is to *SCOREing* a self-compliment. It is simple, but extremely beneficial.

—End of *SCOREing* Approach #14

To those who are deeply indoctrinated into the "Oh, it was no big deal" mode of thinking and are reluctant to switch to *SCOREing* self-complimenting, you may want to think about the following:

Of all the people you will know in your entire lifetime, you are the only one you can never leave nor lose. And you are the one responsible for overcoming the challenges in your life. You are also the one responsible for finding answers to the questions of your life.

The above paragraph is pure truth. The message is clear. You need to take charge of you. There's no question about it—you are fully responsible for yourself and how you handle your circumstances. So accept responsibility now. Start feeding your self-esteem by *SCOREing* a self-compliment for a job well done or a positive quality you have. You do not have to clear all the bad guys out of town, so to speak, before you deserve a self-compliment. You don't need to wait until you do something of incredible magnitude. It is daily handling the little everyday situations that you need to self-compliment because, as wonderful as those around you may be, most people don't compliment others enough, if at all.

Here are a couple of examples on how and when to compliment yourself:

1. You are driving your new car alone for the first time on a remote, little-traveled country road when you get a flat tire. You have never changed a tire before in your life. You are not even certain where the spare tire and tools are. It takes you over an hour, but you manage to change the tire successfully. That certainly deserves *SCOREing* the self-compliment, "You did a good job, (your name)."
2. You pull into a shopping mall parking lot, and notice a parked vehicle with its lights on. You check the vehicle door. If it is unlocked, you open the door and turn off the lights. If the

door is locked, you write down the vehicle's description and license plate number. You give the information to someone in the mall office so an announcement can be made over the public address system. *SCORE* yourself a self-compliment for this, "You did a good job, (your name)."

There are opportunities every day to *SCORE* a self-compliment. You were patient with your children when you would rather have screamed at them. You were patient with coworkers when you wanted to yell at them. You kept going until you reached your goal, even though you felt like quitting. You went straight home from work to be with your family, even though your buddies wanted you to play a round of golf with them. You made some phone calls to prospects when you didn't feel like it. These are all excellent chances for *SCOREing* self-compliments. And you can easily come up with many more.

Start complimenting yourself now for the good things you do, and continue doing so everyday—by *SCOREing*. To help get you started, sincerely say to yourself, "I'm doing a great thing for myself by reading and applying the ideas in this book."

-13-

Look Mom,
No Hands!
Open Your Creativity Channel
by *SCOREing*

*"Cruel and brutal, or loving and generous, the kind of world
you see will determine the quality of people and experiences which
fill your life. In either case, your expectations will be fulfilled."*
—Bruce Garrabrandt—

Remember when you learned to ride a bicycle? Once you mastered basic balancing and turning, you rode without holding onto the handle bars. When you achieved that, you rode by your house holding your hands above your head shouting, "Look, Mom! No hands!" After that, you were probably pleased with yourself enough that you may not have progressed any further. You may not have learned to ride on the rear wheel while holding the front wheel high off the ground. You probably didn't learn to spin around on the rear wheel, or jump or dance with your bike. Your creativity likely stopped with "Look, Mom! No hands!"

Riding with no hands is risky but not difficult. Almost anyone can do it. It requires a little creativity, but not much. But isn't that the way most of us go through life? We use a tiny bit of creativity—just enough to get by—and that's the end of it. What a shame! An infinite amount of creativity is available to all of us *whenever* we ask for it. In a moment I will show you how to bring it out with *SCOREing*.

The only essential difference between you and more successful people is that they have asked for more success and then did whatever it took to achieve it. The conclusion is clear: Do more (of the right things of course), and you, too, can become more successful. But, to do more usually requires some creativity. The problem is, most people equate creativity with being an actor, a musician, a composer, a writer, an inventor, an artist, or a poet. Yes, these are certainly obvious examples of creativity, but creativity encompasses much more than these easily identifiable and perhaps notable endeavors. Doing needlepoint is creative. So is woodworking, clothing design, gourmet cooking, overcoming obstacles, and building a business, just to name a few more.

Whenever you extend your intelligence to cause something to become reality, you are being creative. Probably the most common example of creativity is in overcoming an obstacle that threatens to stand in the way of achieving your dream or goal. For example, for hundreds of years, it was considered impossible to mass produce clothing. But Elias Howe studied the challenge and then created the sewing machine as a solution. Mulligan stew was probably created by someone who had a few odds and ends of various foods. He or she was hungry, studied the situation, and became creative. Participating in crafts and hobbies are other expressions of creativity that are quite common.

Every time you do something creative you become more of a person than you were before. That is just what creativity does for us. It brings out and reinforces the best in you. It does not make any difference whether you write a book, build a business, create a new casserole dish, or negotiate a peace treaty. It is all creative, and you'll benefit personally for having done so.

Every one of us has the ability to be more creative than we currently are. We have the capacity to extend our intelligence to bring something into reality that does not currently exist. Our subconscious mind, which is our obedient servant, will furnish us with whatever creativity we need or can handle. All we need to do is ask. And, of course, we can ask by *SCOREing*. Everything I have ever written was done in a *SCOREing* "consultation" with my subconscious mind. By asking I received, and therefore developed personally.

When I first started talking out loud to myself, I believed my subconscious was intelligent. I promptly named it "Clyde" and always addressed my *SCOREing* talk to Clyde. "Clyde, I have a challenge," I would begin, and then I'd state what I wanted to do. I got help 100 percent of the time!

SCOREing Approach #15—*Talking to Your Subconscious*

You could start out this way: "I desire to talk directly with my subconscious mind on an ongoing basis from now on for the rest of my life. To make communication easier, I am naming my subconscious mind (state any name you choose)." For illustration purposes, I will use the name Clyde.

"Clyde, I need your help and want your help to open up all of my creativity so I can do more and become all I was created to be. I want to be more creative. Help me, please."

After that initial appeal, talk to Clyde as often as you wish about anything you want for the rest of your life. Just always start out by addressing your subconscious mind by name (i.e., "Clyde, I have come to consult with you") in order to establish a solid, direct line of communication. Then watch what wonderful things happen in your life as you go forward in faith and take action. You will be amazed.

—End of *SCOREing* Approach #15

Of course, if your subconscious gives you creative ideas and you ignore them, the ideas will cease to be given to you. It's the old "cry wolf" syndrome. So be serious about this. As it says in the Bible, "Ask and you shall receive." Beyond that, though, you need to act upon it if you really want to make progress. Now you can open up your creativity by *SCOREing*. The ball is in your court. Play the game by making the next move.

"*We all have only one life to live, and I have no intention of wasting a single moment in a vacuum waiting for something to happen. How about you? I believe in making things happen because that's what makes life exciting and fulfilling.*"

—Bill Wayne

-14-

Too Much Time on Your Hands?
Use Time Constructively With *SCOREing*

*"Know the true value of time; snatch, seize, and enjoy
every moment of it. No idleness, no laziness, no procrastination:
Never put off till tomorrow what you can do today."*
—Lord Chesterfield—

I am never completely idle because I don't like doing nothing. By idle, I mean having absolutely nothing to play at, work at, read, study, plan, watch, or listen to. It means just hanging around waiting for something to happen to fill the time. I have no tolerance for idleness. We all have only one life to live, and I have no intention of wasting a single moment in a vacuum waiting for something to happen. How about you?

I believe in making things happen because that's what makes life exciting and fulfilling. But it wasn't always like this for me. Years ago, I had plenty of "hanging around" time, which actually used to tire me out. Doing nothing, especially when this is a regularly occurring state, can be a very tiresome "activity". This is probably due to the frustration that comes because nothing generally happens—nothing that you want to happen, that is.

As I grew, I discovered how *SCOREing* could fill my time completely, enjoyably, and satisfyingly. I used *SCOREing* to discover what I needed to do next when I didn't know what to do. I use the same *SCOREing* technique after I finish writing something and don't know what to write about next. It works every time.

The approach is simple. Think about this: What would you do if someone came to you, such as a son or daughter, and said, "I'm bored. I don't have anything to do"? You could help them by asking questions that could lead to his or her finding something to do. Your questions might include: "Is your homework done yet? Did you clean up your room yet? Do you have a book to read? Why not finish that model airplane you started building last month? How about writing a letter to Grandma? Why not give Jack a call? Would you like to shoot some hoops with me down at the school or go shopping with Mom at the mall? And so forth…"

Now go ahead and do exactly the same thing with yourself. Help yourself find the best thing for you to do, for example, to reach one of your goals. Just think of some pertinent questions and ask them of yourself out loud—then answer them to yourself out loud. For example, you could ask yourself, "What is the most important thing I can do right now to build my business or career? What have I been procrastinating about that really needs to be done? Who do I need to call or see? Where do I need to go?" It is surprising how quickly you can come up with an answer when you focus by asking yourself questions.

You can creatively meet and overcome challenges the same way. An example scenario might go something like this, remembering that all questioning and answering is to be done *out loud to yourself*:

SCOREing Approach #16A—*Solving a Problem*

You are driving an 18-wheeler truck and, because of a detour, you find yourself on an unfamiliar narrow country road. You are approaching an overpass labeled Clearance 12' 11". You know your rig is slightly less than 13' 0" but you don't think it is a full inch less, so you brake to a stop. A quick glance tells you that you will tear the roof off the trailer if you try to go under the overpass. So you start *SCOREing* as follows:

Q: "Now what do I need to do?"
A: "I could turn around and go back and take another route."
Q: "But how am I going to do that? This narrow road has no shoulders and there is a deep ditch on each side."
A: "Right. There is no way I can turn this rig around here."

Q: "Would it be best to put out some flares and wait for help?"
A: "I could do that, I suppose. Or maybe I could get someone on the CB."

Q: "Why not check closely to see exactly how much more clearance is needed?"
A: "Okay." You then ease the rig up so the front edge of the trailer is nearly touching the bottom of the overpass.

Q: "How much more clearance is needed?"
A: "About a quarter inch," you answer after sizing it up.

Q: "So why not lower the rig about a half inch by letting some air out of the tires? I can refill the tires at the next service station I come to."
A: "Good idea. I'll do it."

You solved the problem by using *SCOREing* to repeatedly ask yourself questions and examine options. This is a simplistic example, but it effectively illustrates the process.

—End of *SCOREing* Approach #16A

This process helps to work through challenges, flush out fresh ideas, or come up with an idea if you are ever uncertain about what you need to do next. *SCOREing* is always simple. You just meet the situation head-on by talking it over out loud with yourself. Ask simple, direct questions and give simple, direct answers—and you will lead yourself to exactly where you want to be. Much can be done toward whatever it is you wish to accomplish during usually wasted waiting time.

SCOREing Approach #16B—*Using Waiting Time Wisely*

It is 2 p.m. You have two hours before leaving for the airport to pick up your spouse.

Q: "What can I do for two hours?"

A: "Go to the airport early and just hang around."

Q: "No. I want something constructive to do. Tell me what to do."

A: "Watch the people."

Q: "No. That'll just pass the time, but I won't accomplish anything."

A: "Then read a book or a magazine."

Q: "I've read the magazines already and I could read a book, but I want to take advantage of the fact that there are a lot of people in the airport. Give me a project that will take one to two hours. Okay?"

A: "How about setting a goal to meet and talk with three or four people who could potentially be new business prospects? Go make some new friends!"

Q: "Hmm? Is that a great idea or what?"

A: "Okay. I'll do it. Thanks."

— End of *SCOREing* Approach #16B

You are probably wondering why you need to go through these conversations out loud to yourself. "Why can't I just do it silently in my head?" you may ask. Well, you could do it in your head, but you're less likely to get the quick, solid results you would like to have. Concentration is much greater when you talk out loud to yourself. When you just think about these things, your mind can be easily distracted. You are quite likely to end up just having a rambling daydreaming session rather than arriving at any concrete conclusions and achieving constructive results. Remember in an earlier chapter when we discussed how your mind can be like a stubborn child?

When you talk out loud to yourself, you cause yourself to superfocus on the challenge, situation, or circumstances. This activity increases the likelihood of obtaining a desirable solution much more quickly. It is easy to daydream nonproductively for an hour or two, but it only wastes time and doesn't give you the results you would like to have. It is incredibly powerful hearing your own voice proclaiming what you want to accomplish. A little talking out loud to yourself can go a long way.

"**D**on't tell me you don't have the time. That's just an excuse. Everyone on earth has 24 hours a day—no more, no less. All the pictures ever painted, all the books ever written, all the inventions ever created, and all the businesses ever built were done by men and women who have only 24 hours in a day. So don't cry to me, 'I don't have time.'"

—Bill Wayne

-15-

Don't Settle for Might-Have-Been Dreams

SCOREing to Set Priorities

"We should all be concerned about the future because we will have to spend the rest of our lives there."
—Charles F. Kettering—

I have a friend who is a talented artist, but you wouldn't know it because he doesn't paint very often. He simply hasn't established his priorities to use his time as he would like. He spends 40 hours a week earning a living at a mundane, non-art-related job. Then, of course, he has the usual things to do around the house: weeding the flower beds, tending to the lawn, and painting his sun-bleached siding. There are also the customary repair jobs like fussing with sticking doors and cracked tiles, as well as stopping leaks in the plumbing.

Funny thing though, he doesn't get around to the household chores either. He has so many other things to do and, after all, there are only 24 hours in a day. He also needs to eat and sleep. What other things?

Most weekends there is a party or two—always something to celebrate. Every weekday evening he watches television, starting with the 6:30 p.m. television world news, straight through until 11:30 p.m. at the end of the local news. Then he drags his weary body off to bed—so he can get up early the next morning and go to the job he hates for one reason or another. Of course, then there are, according to him, "must-see" programs that he absolutely won't miss. If he's bored with T.V., he plays on the Internet for awhile—flitting from one web site to the next—just to pass the time. Amazingly, he *does* have time to do these things. So there just isn't enough time to paint, too, and he constantly bemoans it: "I love to paint, but I never seem to have the time."

I have said to him, "That's just an excuse. Everyone on earth has 24 hours in a day—no more, no less. All the pictures ever painted, all the books ever written, all the inventions ever created, and all the businesses ever built were done by men and women who have only 24 hours in a day. So don't cry to me 'I don't have time.'" The truth is, we can all find the time to do whatever it is we really want to do. A key secret to success is to make maximum use of your time by setting and sticking to *priorities*.

My wife crochets afghans while watching TV and does needlework on long airplane rides. She maximizes the use of her time by doing something she loves to do. And my would-be-artist friend *could* paint a picture a week, if he wanted to badly enough. If a painting required ten hours' work, he could trade off two hours of TV watching or net surfing each night for five consecutive nights. It is just a matter of *firmly* setting priorities and then *doggedly* sticking to them.

You have already learned one way to make maximum use of your time through *SCOREing* while taking a shower or while you're in your vehicle stopped for a traffic light, and so forth. *SCOREing* can also help you set and stick to your priorities. Perhaps if you have a challenge similar to my artist friend—Approach #17 is based on his situation:

SCOREing Approach #17—*Setting a Priority*

"I am going to paint a mountain scene this week which will take me about ten hours. I am determined to do this and I shall discipline myself to do it. I shall paint from 6 p.m. until 8 p.m.

every evening until I am 100 percent finished. No matter *what* is on TV at that time or how much I might be tempted to turn on my computer, I will paint my mountain scene. That is my painting time. And if I feel like painting beyond 8 p.m., I shall. However, I will not stop painting until I have put in at least two full hours every evening. I will find reasons to paint rather than make excuses for not painting. I will paint because that is truly what I want to do. It is my number one priority."

— End of *SCOREing* Approach #17

Use Approach #17 as a model to create a similar approach for whatever your particular priority challenge is. Then *SCORE* it daily until you have successfully made the priority a part of your life so it is no longer pushed aside.

John Greenleaf Whittier once wrote—"For of all the sad words of tongue and pen, the saddest are these: It might have been!" Don't let your life's dreams become might-have-beens. Change the potential sadness of "It might have been" into the living joy of actual achievement by *SCOREing* daily to set and execute your priorities.

I have shared what's in this chapter with my artist friend. Did it work for him? Well, no. He didn't make *SCOREing* a priority and left himself with no time to do it! What can I say? Sometimes people just seem to be satisfied dreaming about a life that might have been instead living one that *is*. But it doesn't have to be that way—for anyone! My hope is that *you* will make *SCOREing* a priority and create a wonderful life for yourself, that *is*—not just one that "might have been."

"**F**ollow the beat of a different drummer. Start talking out loud to yourself and march to your own tune by SCOREing. Follow your dream and it'll take you wherever you're supposed to go...."

—Bill Wayne

-16-

Do You Hear the Beat of a Different Drummer?
March to Your Own Tune by *SCOREing*

"If a man fails to keep pace with his companions, perhaps it is because he hears a different drummer. Let him step to the music he hears, however measured or far away."
—Henry David Thoreau—

In the above quotation, Thoreau was wisely stating that people who consciously make their own choices, who deliberately set out to determine their own destiny and march to their own tune in life, need to be allowed—and encouraged—to do so. The implication could be, and correctly so, that the world is a better place for having people who listen to and follow a different drummer.

Thoreau also wrote that "The masses of men lead lives of quiet desperation." But you may have noticed that people aren't so quiet about it these days. They often believe they are victims who are entitled to a better life. They don't take responsibility for the life they've created and often complain about how the world has treated them. Thoreau was sharing his observation that most people lead unfulfilling, low-achievement lives simply because they march to the beat of someone else's drummer rather than to the beat of their own. This often shows up in the humdrum job routine they've gotten themselves into, working for someone else's dream instead of their own.

Scoring Scenario: Here's a sample scenario of someone who let himself become a slave to his father's dream rather than marching to the beat of his own drummer. It is followed by *SCOREing* Approach #18, which can be used to help people in a similar situation break free of the thinking and behaviors that got them there. It'll help you think for yourself and act accordingly.

Chad, a man in his late 30s, was feeling disappointed about the sad state of his career. He had gone to college for accounting because his father was an accountant and wanted Chad to follow in his footsteps. His dad owned an accounting firm, and Chad had been working for him since he graduated from college at age 22. The problem was, it was getting harder and harder for Chad to get up in the morning and go to work. He found accounting work tedious and boring. He really wanted to have his own business, but just couldn't quite muster the courage to get started.

SCOREing Approach #18—*Becoming a Business Owner*

Q: "Chad, you're not happy with your career, are you?"
A: "No, I'm terribly unhappy."

Q: "What would you *really, really* like to do?
A: "I'd like to be financially free and have more time to do the things I want to do."

Q: "So what's holding you back? Is it lack of money?"
A: "No. In fact, Jeff down the street has asked me to associate with him in his business, which he's very excited about."

Q: "Chad, once again, what's holding you back?"
A: "Well, the truth is, I'll be letting Dad down. He's depending on me."

Q: "You would need to work your day job, anyway, a while longer as you build your business, right?"

A: "Yeah, I can't afford to do it any other way. And even if I could, Jeff doesn't recommend it."

Q: "Have you ever considered the idea that your dad might be burned out with accounting and may himself be interested in associating with you in your new business?"
A: "Come to think of it, Dad has been complaining more than ever about his business. In fact, he's been really testy lately—it's not like him. Maybe he's ready for a change."

Q: "Anything else holding you back?"
A: "No."

Q: "Great. Then will you go for it?"
A: "Yes, thanks!"
                                    —End of *SCOREing* Approach #18

SCOREing is a tool you can use to write your own "musical composition" in life. It better enables you to be your own drummer and march to your own tune. In addition to the approach just covered, you can write your own tune using various approaches. This book doesn't cover all the possibilities and potentials of *SCOREing,* but it offers a great place to start.

As you use *SCOREing* in more areas of your life, you will undoubtedly develop your own unique methods and purposes. Follow the beat of a different drummer. Start talking out loud to yourself and march to your own tune by *SCOREing*. Follow your dream and it'll take you wherever you're supposed to go....

"**W**ho cares what others may think? They're not paying my bills, and they don't know what dreams and goals I have inside of me. Doing something different is the right and necessary thing for me to do. So I'll do it regardless of what anyone else may think!"

—Bill Wayne

-17-

Climb to the Tippity Top
My Hopes for Your *SCOREing* Success

*"The rung of a ladder was never meant to rest upon,
but only to hold a man's foot long enough to enable him
to put the other somewhat higher."*
—Thomas Henry Huxley—

Many decades ago, when I was a senior in high school, I took a competitive college scholarship examination. The test took all day, and some 300 students participated. The one person with the top score was to be awarded a full four-year scholarship to Bowling Green University in Ohio. The next nine would receive an Honorable Mention Certificate, but nothing else. Below the top ten, there would be no award of any kind.

One question on the exam was a heavily weighted three-part essay-type question. We had to identify: 1) the specific literary work; 2) the author of that work; and 3) interpret the meaning of this phrase "Grates me; the sum" from that work. Partially correct answers were counted as being incorrect, and all three parts had to be answered correctly.

I had no idea what the answer could be. It sounded to me like something Shakespeare might have written, but I didn't know which of his works it may have been or what the meaning might be. So I guessed

Shakespeare's *Julius Caesar*, and I thought the sentence meant "Summarize the information for me."

My answer was marked wrong and, unfortunately, I didn't know if I had gotten it even partly correct. I had to settle for an Honorable Mention Certificate, which I threw away in anger at myself for not knowing the right answer. In those youthful days, I hadn't yet learned that even if we do our level best, we're not going to get the desired result a hundred percent of the time.

Ever since then, the meaning of "Grates me; the sum" has puzzled me. Would I have won the scholarship if I had answered that question correctly? Who knows? What does that quote mean? It fascinated me so much that I've always wanted to use it in my speaking and writing. But I didn't feel compelled (until now) to use it because I still didn't know what it meant. So, off and on I used *SCOREing* to lead me to find the answer.

Finally, on November 3, 1998, over 50 years after I had taken that scholarship test, I finally found out the correct answer. The line is from William Shakespeare's play *Antony and Cleopatra,* written in 1607. The words are spoken by Antony in Act 1, Scene 1 in Cleopatra's palace in Alexandria. Cleopatra and Antony are talking when an attendant enters the room and announces: "News, my good lord, from Rome." Antony replies: "Grates me; the sum." In other words, Antony was saying "This irritates me; give me the bottom line."

So it appears that my guess many years ago was two-thirds correct. If I had guessed *Antony and Cleopatra* instead of *Julius Caesar,* I would have gotten credit for answering the question, and maybe I would have won the scholarship! I guess I'll never know. But who cares? It is no longer important. Shortly after high school I enlisted in the Air Force and then later went on to a career in corporate management and then professional writing.

So why am I bringing up this "Grates me; the sum" incident? It may seem like a foolish whim to you, but is it really? Think about it for a moment. I ventured to explore something I did not understand, and in so doing, I feel better about it. Most importantly, I ultimately found the answer I was seeking. I never gave up. I persisted and succeeded. And you can too!

Many people hesitate to explore opportunities to grow because they are fearful of doing something new, and don't quite understand the potential benefits. That's why they usually lead boring, unfulfilling lives. How about you? Have you ever had a fearful attitude about doing something different that could give you the results you want? We may prefer to remain stuck in our conventional ways and not allow ourselves to say, "Who cares what others may think? They're not paying my bills, and they don't know what dreams and goals I have inside of me. Doing something different is the right and necessary thing for me to do. So I'll do it regardless of what anyone else may think!"

How about having this attitude about *SCOREing*? You may not really understand how or why *SCOREing* works, and that's OK, but isn't it worth a shot? Why not? Let go of any attitude you may have about always "playing it safe" and being conventional! Perhaps, for once in your life, you'll loosen up and do something just because *you* want to. Talk out loud to yourself with *SCOREing* and you will feel better about yourself and what it is you want to do. It is an emancipating experience, and it will give you a new sense of freedom.

I suppose I am somewhat of an expert on *SCOREing* but, frankly, I don't fully understand all aspects of it either. I just do it, and it works. I have a great time, and my life keeps getting better, and better, and better.

As people, we are multifaceted beings. There are many aspects to our collective natures. We are emotional, rational, interpersonal, intrapersonal, ambitious, hopeful, goal-seeking, self-appreciating, and we have many opposite corresponding characteristics as well as many more components too extensive to mention. And this book provides a broad spectrum of approaches to cover many of the challenges of life that we all encounter to one degree or another.

One very important aspect, however, that has not been covered yet is *leadership*. What is leadership? What is a leader? There are so many diverse concepts about leadership that a good *SCOREing* approach for becoming a leader could be tailored to each person's concept of what leadership means to him or her.

My dictionary gives 29 definitions for a leader and leadership. And a friend told me that his unabridged dictionary defines leadership in 56 ways! I heard a politician proclaim that a leader is a person who senses where the crowd is headed and then hurries to get out in front! An instructor in a management training class that I attended   years ago said that a leader is a person who studies all the existing paths that might be taken to overcome a challenge, and selects the best path for others to follow. These two definitions are among the 29 in my dictionary, but I personally do not subscribe to either one. I believe a leader is someone who goes where there is no path, leaves a trail for others to follow, and then helps them to succeed.   The world definitely could use more good leaders at every level of society.

If you aspire to leadership, use the *SCOREing* approaches you have learned about to create your own approach in attaining the role to which you aspire. Ask yourself enough questions for you to come out with the best answers for you. Here's an approach to help stir your thinking about becoming a leader:

SCOREing Approach #19—*Becoming a Leader*

Q: "Why would I want to become a leader?"

A: "Well, to be perfectly frank and open, leaders, at least in business, often make more money!"

Q: "Are you in any way uncomfortable with that fact?"

A: "I used to think having a lot of money was wrong, but now I'm not sure."

Q: "How come you're uncertain?"

A: "Isn't money evil?"

Q: "No, it's the *love* of money that's evil. Money is just a tool we use as a medium of exchange. It builds churches and schools, buys food, puts clothes on our backs and roofs over our heads. People with negative intentions do destructive things with some of their money, but people with good intentions are more likely to do good things with theirs. Some people say money is evil—so they can use it as an excuse not to change their unproductive ways. Money isn't a luxury either. In fact, it's as necessary as oxygen."

A: "I've got to admit that, for most of my life, I've pretty much just maintained my position rather than moved ahead. I guess I've been a follower, rather than a leader. Part of me said that if I were a leader and started making lots of money, I'd become materialistic."

Q: "Lots of people don't really gain success and momentum and grow into leaders until they are somewhat older and wiser. Like many of them, maybe you just needed your younger years to grow to this turning point. What do you think? Could you be one of these so-called late bloomers?"
A: "I suppose so. But this materialism thing still bothers me."

Q: "I understand. Have you ever noticed that those people most focused on the material things in life are the folks who don't have much money? They're often trying so hard to look good—as if they do have money—that they nearly drown in interest payments on their loans and finance charges on their credit cards. They become broker and broker. They're often the followers rather than the leaders. Did you know that Sam Walton, the founder of Wal-Mart and Sam's Club stores, drove around in an old pickup truck? He was a leader with considerable wealth, but he was not materialistic. And you don't have to be either. Go ahead and stretch your wings—learn to be a leader. We can talk again anytime you need to."
A: "Okay, thanks. I'm going to muster up my courage and go for it."

—End of *SCOREing* Approach #19

My hope is that there is something in this book to help everyone. My hope is that you will get a good enough feel for *SCOREing* to be able to devise your own approaches for any situation not specifically covered in this book. My hope is that you will take the plunge and start *SCOREing* every day for your own benefit. In doing so, you can climb to the peak of success and fulfillment, while taking others along with you, too, as they observe the positive changes in your life!

"There comes a time when you need to stop talking, release the matter, gather your confidence, go forward, and make things happen."

—Bill Wayne

-18-

When to Stop Talking
When to Stop *SCOREing* and Relax

"The first law of success...is concentration. Blend all the energies to one point—focus—and go directly to that point, looking neither to the right nor the left."
—William Matthews—

For 17 chapters now you've been encouraged to give your mouth a verbal workout—to talk, and talk, and talk incessantly out loud to yourself. But, do you need to continue talking on the same subject forever? No, you don't. Do you need to continue talking on the same subject until you achieve a hundred percent of the results you want? No, you don't. There comes a time when you need to stop talking, and in this chapter I will tell you when and why. It all has to do with the *Law of Focus,* which states:

"Whatever happens to you, whatever comes to you, whatever surrounds you will be in accordance with your focus and nothing else. That whatever you focus on shall happen no matter who tries to stop it. And if you do not focus on what you want, you cannot possibly attain it."

The *Law of Focus* is a simple pure truth: What you keep putting into your mind you will eventually achieve—as long as you continuously take action on your thoughts. Conversely, nothing in, nothing out. Nothing ventured, nothing gained. The whole purpose of the various *SCOREing* approaches is to help you program your subconscious with exactly what you want in it for various situations. Once the ideas are installed, there's no need to program the same material again, for your mind will have already absorbed it. After that, you can count on it to support you in making things happen at the right time and in the right way for your best interests. Once you have a *SCOREing* scenario and approach firmly programmed into your subconscious and your thinking and behavior has changed to reflect it, it is time to stop talking on that particular scenario. Relax with it and move on to something else.

There will be times when you perform a scenario only once, and get immediate results. An example could be releasing frustration as described in Chapter 11. A frustration may have recently entered your mind, but with one emotional *SCOREing* session you may be able to turn your attitude around and remove its harmful effects. Remember, when you *SCORE with emotion* you can create deeper and faster programming, thus getting quicker, more solid results. Emotion affects the subconscious in a most powerful way.

Other times you may need to use a *SCOREing* approach for more extended periods before you have programmed your subconscious mind sufficiently. An example is to stop smoking as described in Chapter 5. The smoking habit may have been deeply programmed into your subconscious over a long period of time. Therefore, it will most likely take some time and persistence to reprogram yourself to become a nonsmoker.

However, you do not necessarily need to achieve a hundred percent desired results before you stop your *SCOREing* for a particular purpose. Maybe a small improvement in that area is all you need. Once you feel you have programmed your mind sufficiently, and you are satisfied with your progress, stop talking and release the matter.

Sometimes you'll get results so fast that you know you have succeeded with your programming. At that point, just stop talking! But what if results do not happen as fast as you'd like? Until you have a sense of completion with your programming and know that you're on track, keep up the *SCOREing*. Don't stop until you feel satisfied.

For years, I programmed myself daily that I wanted to become a successful author. I had no rational reason to believe that I could, or should, write books. But that is what I wanted to do, so I used *SCOREing* for that purpose. Then, one day I had a quiet, confident awareness deep inside that my subconscious was permanently programmed for me to be an author. At that point, I still had not written a book of any sort and had no idea what to write about. Yet I knew, in my heart, that it would happen. I immediately stopped *SCOREing* for that specific purpose because *I knew* it was now in my mind, and therefore would happen. It must happen, because that is the *Law of Focus*. So I relaxed with it, released my thoughts of being an author, and went on to think about and do other things.

Once I had stopped *SCOREing,* relaxed with it and let it go, things happened fast. Within two weeks the entire concept for a book came into my mind—seemingly out of nowhere. I sat down at the keyboard and began to write. The words came almost faster than I could type. In 30 days I had written the complete manuscript, and the concept for a second book had already entered my mind. I immediately started writing the second book. "All of a sudden" I was off and running as an author because it was deeply imbedded in my mind that that's what I was supposed to do!

There comes a time when you need to stop talking, release the matter, gather your confidence, go forward, and make things happen. You'll know when to stop talking and why. Now *I* will stop talking. It's your turn to *SCORE* and create more success-inducing habits. As Fulton Sheen said...

"*The great advantage of habit is that it saves us a lot of attention, effort, and brainwork.*"

Who Is Bill Wayne?

After serving six years in the U.S. Air Force, Bill joined a major manufacturer of computers as a technical writer. He quickly received a series of promotions that took him into executive management in charge of the company's technical publications department. He was sent to some of the best management schools in the country, and began learning what success is all about, forming his own philosophy. He resigned from the computer company after 18 years to pursue a professional writing career contracting his skills to a wide variety of corporations. All of his work entailed working with engineers and professional managers, where Bill further enhanced and developed his knowledge of what it takes to be a success.

After Bill retired, he reflected on his career and put together his unique approach to helping others get ahead in life. The result of his life's work is this book—*The Power of Talking Out Loud to Yourself.* It brings one aspect of his knowledge to a wide range of readers, giving them another tool they can use to accelerate their own success.